FUTURE
English for Results

1

MULTILEVEL COMMUNICATIVE ACTIVITIES BOOK

Sarah Lynn

Series Consultants
Beatriz B. Díaz
Ronna Magy
Federico Salas-Isnardi

PEARSON
Longman

Future 1 Multilevel Communicative Activities
English for Results

Pearson Education, 10 Bank Street, White Plains, NY 10606

Staff credits: The people who made up the *Future 1 MCA* team, representing editorial, production, design, and manufacturing, are Jennifer Adamec, Elizabeth Carlson, Nancy Flaggman, Irene Frankel, Michael Kemper, Melissa Leyva, Michael Mone, Liza Pleva, and Barbara Sabella.

Cover design: Rhea Banker
Text design: Wanda España
Text composition: Rainbow Graphics
Text font: 13 pt Minion
Illustrations: Steve Attoe, pp. 9, 75, 83; Kenneth Batelman, p. 61; Pierre Berthiaume, pp. 17, 55, 97; Laurie Conley, pp. 7, 25, 35, 91, 105; Deborah Crowle, p. 3; Scott Fray, p. 41; Brian Hughes, pp. 31, 53, 93, 101; Andrew Meyer, pp. 39, 87; Allan Moon, p. 33; Phil Scheuer, pp. 49, 59, 67, 117; Neil Stewart, p. 57.

ISBN-13: 978-0-13-199146-0
ISBN-10: 0-13-199146-9

PEARSON LONGMAN ON THE **WEB**

Pearsonlongman.com offers online resources for teachers and students. Access our Companion Websites, our online catalog, and our local offices around the world.

Visit us at **pearsonlongman.com**.

Printed in the United States of America
1 2 3 4 5 6 7 8 9 10—DME—14 13 12 11 10 09

Contents

Unit 7 Day After Day

Introduction

Welcome to the *Future 1 Multilevel Communicative Activities Book.*

The *Future 1 Multilevel Communicative Activities Book* contains 60 communicative ready-to-use reproducible activities. Each activity corresponds to a lesson in the Student Book and recycles the vocabulary, language structures, and themes of that lesson. The activities are a valuable addition to the class, focusing on fun and communication while helping students internalize the new target language.

Each activity is accompanied by detailed teacher notes that step the teacher through the activity and provide suggestions for adapting the activity to multilevel students in the same classroom. Very little teacher preparation time is needed, and the only additional materials needed are a photocopier and a pair of scissors.

What makes the activities in the book communicative?

All of the activities require students to communicate effectively to accomplish a task. The task may be to share information with a partner to complete a bus schedule or to walk around the classroom to ask their classmates about their weekend plans. The activities are highly structured ensuring that students always know what they need to do and how close they are to accomplishing the task.

What makes the activities multilevel?

Adult Ed ESL classrooms are by nature multilevel. Many factors—including the student's age, educational background, and literacy level—contribute to the student's level. In fact, the same student may be *at level* in one skill, but *pre-level* or *above-level* in another. The greatest challenge for a teacher of a multilevel class is to keep all the students engaged all the time, drawing on their strengths and supporting them through their weak areas.

The teacher notes include Multilevel Options so teachers can adapt the activities for pre-level and above-level learners. They offer specific ways to provide the pre-level students with additional scaffolding for extra support and to challenge the above-level learners to work more independently and to extend the activity.

How do the activities engage all the students?

The activities in this book engage learners in a number of ways. First, nearly all the activities integrate all four language skills: speaking, listening, reading, and writing. Second, the activities involve different learning modalities. For example, many activities have students move as they learn and will appeal to kinesthetic learners. Many activities require students to interpret graphs, maps, game boards, and pictures and will appeal to visual learners. Third, the activities encourage students of all levels to contribute. The responsibilities for a task are distributed so that everyone must participate and everyone must give feedback. No students are left out. All learners contribute what they can based on their strengths and receive the multilayered scaffolding support to help them in their weaker areas. Because the activities are highly interactive and dynamic, they provide learners with many opportunities to negotiate meaning and check comprehension. This keeps the class humming with energy and purposeful communication.

Overview of Activity Types

Activity	Grouping	Task
Board Game	Small Groups	Students play a board that reviews unit theme, grammar structures, and vocabulary.
Build a Sentence	Pairs	Students assemble words and phrases into meaningful sentences.
Drawing Game	Pairs	One partner describes a scene as the other partner listens and draws the scene. Then they switch roles.
Find Someone Who	Whole-Class Mixer	Students ask their classmates questions in order to complete a series of sentences.
Give and Take Game	Whole-Class Mixer	Students barter items so everyone in the class can get what they need.
Information Gap	Pairs	Students ask and answer questions in order to find missing information in everyday print formats such as receipts, bus schedules, weather maps, and job applications.
Interview	Pairs	In sustained conversation, students ask each other a series of questions and report their findings to the class.
Matching Game	Whole-Class Mixer	Students ask and answer questions about their cards to find the correct match.
Miming Game	Pairs	Students give clues to words by acting out their meaning.
Picture Match	Whole-Class Mixer	Students ask and answer questions about their pictures to find their match.
Picture-based Story	Whole Class and Pairs	Together the class composes a story based on a picture that reflects on one of the unit's themes.
Question and Answer Game	Small Groups or Pairs	Students ask and answer questions using visual cues such as a map or realia in the classroom.
Survey	Whole-Class Mixer	Students ask their fellow classmates a question and report the results.
Tic-Tac-Toe	Small Groups	Teams play the classic game with a new twist; they must compose correct questions about their classmates to score a box in the grid.

About the Teacher Notes

Teacher Notes

Teacher Notes appear on the page facing each Activity Master and provide comprehensive instructions and lesson planning ideas.

> A **cross-reference** to the Student Book indicates after which page in the Student Book the activity should be done.

> Teachers can see at a glance how to set up the class and plan the lesson.

> **Teacher Preparation** lists what the teacher needs to do before the class.

> **Procedure** guides the teacher, step-by-step through the activity.

> **Multilevel Options** suggest simple ways a teacher can adapt an activity for pre-level and/or above-level students.

> **Extension** provides the teacher with additional ideas for extending the activity.

> **Variation** suggests an alternative approach to the activity.

Unit 2 · Lesson 8

→ **Future 1 pages 40–41**

Find Someone Who: *Jobs and Workplaces*

Grouping Whole-class mixer
Target Language Jobs, workplaces
Materials Activity Master 9
Class Time 20 minutes

Teacher Preparation

- Copy Activity Master 9, one for each student.
- Cut out the chart on each copy. Cut enough cards so that each student has an occupation.

Procedure

1. Give each student a copy of the chart and a card with an occupation. Give an above-level student the card with *cook* as the occupation. You'll need to call on the student when you model the activity in step 3 below.

2. Explain that students are going to pretend that the occupation on their card is their real-life occupation. Tell them that they will walk around the classroom. They will ask and answer *What do you do?* and *Where do you work?* in order to complete as many sentences in the chart as possible. Tell students they will have 15 minutes for the activity.

3. Write *What do you do? Where do you work?* on the board. Play the part of Student A. Walk around the classroom. Stop at the desk of the student you gave the card to. Have him or her play the part of Student B. Model the conversation:

    A: *What do you do?*

    B: *I'm a cook.*

    A: *Where do you work?*

    B: (Looks at chart and chooses correct workplace) *I work at a restaurant.*

    A: (Writes students name next to *works at a restaurant* in the chart)

4. To give students more support, write the model conversation on the board.

5. Circulate during the activity to help students formulate questions and answers correctly.

Multilevel Options

Pre-level: If pre-level students have difficulty writing their classmates' names, allow them to ask: *Can you write that for me please?* Also have pre-level students refer to the conversation on the board.

Above-level: Challenge above-level students to do the activity without looking at the board.

Extension

After the class has finished the activity, write the occupations on the board. Instruct students to match the occupations with the workplaces. Write their answers on the board. Tell students that some occupations might have more than one possible workplace. For example, a cashier could work at a restaurant or a store.

Variation

Have students do the activity in groups of 4. After five minutes, have students read aloud their sentences. The rest of the class listens and completes Activity Master 9.

The World Map: *Where are you from?*

Grouping	Whole-class mixer
Target Language	Reading a map, country names
Materials	Activity Master 1
Class Time	20 minutes

Teacher Preparation

Copy Activity Master 1, one for each student.

Procedure

1. Give a copy of Activity Master 1 to each student.

2. Explain that students are going to walk around the classroom to write information on a world map. Students will ask each other where they are from. Each will point out his or her country on the map on Activity Master 1 and then write the name of his or her country on the map. Tell students they will have 15 minutes for the activity.

3. Play the part of Student A. Walk around the classroom. Ask above-level students to play the parts of Student B and Student C. Then model the activity:

    A: *Where are you from?* (Shows student his or her map)

    B: *I'm from* _____. (Points to his or her country on the map)

    A: *Can you write that for me, please?*

    B: (Writes country on A's map and draws a line connecting his or her name to the country)

    A: (Questions another student) *Where are you from?* (Shows student his or her map)

    C: *I'm from* _____. (Points to his or her country on the map)

    A: *Can you write that for me, please?*

    C: (Writes country on A's map and draws a line connecting the name to the country)

4. To give students more support, write the model conversation on the board.

5. Circulate during the activity to help students find their home countries on the map and write their country names in appropriately small letters.

6. After 15 minutes, ask students to read the country names written on their individual maps. Write all the country names on the board and make sure students can find the countries on their map.

Multilevel Option

Pre-level: Have pre-level students refer to the map on pages 6 and 7 in their Student Book for help in locating their own country on Activity Master 1.

Variation

If all the students in your class are from one country, use Activity Master 1 to reinforce students' knowledge of country names. Put students in like-ability pairs and give each pair a copy of Activity Master 1. Set a 7-minute time limit and have students write on the map the names of all the countries they know. After time is up, have each pair read their list of country names to the class and show where each country is located on the map.

Extension

If some students finish before the rest of the class, have them unscramble the following country names:

adacan (Canada)
dneagln (England)
itunde esatst (United States)
srsiau (Russia)

Remind them to capitalize the first letter of each country.

The World Map: *Where are you from?*

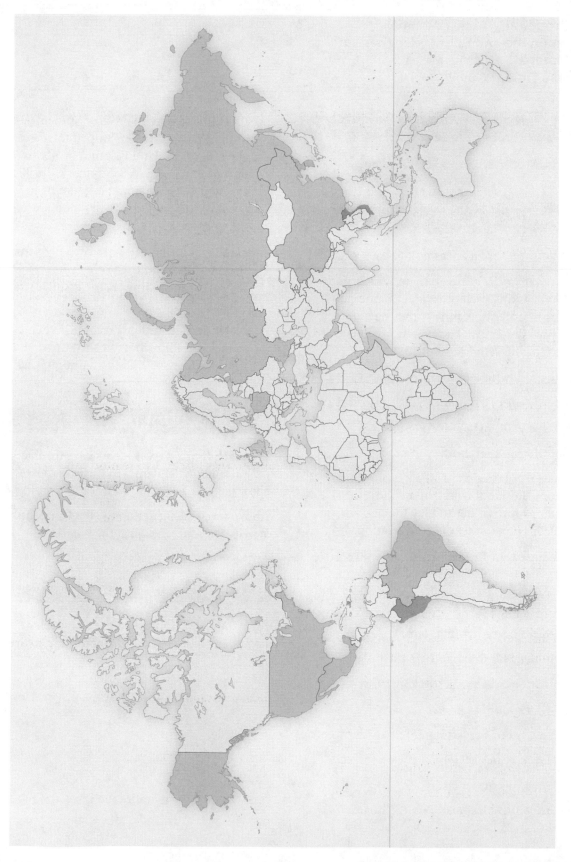

Unit 1 • Lesson 3

Survey: *How do you spell that?*

Grouping	Whole-class mixer
Target Language	Alphabet, spelling names
Materials	Activity Master 2
Class Time	20 minutes

Teacher Preparation

Copy Activity Master 2, one for each student.

Procedure

1. Give a copy of Activity Master 2 to each student.

2. Explain that students are going to walk around the classroom, asking each other their names and spellings in order to complete the chart on Activity Master 2. Tell students they will have 15 minutes for the activity.

3. Write the following questions on the board:

   What's your first name?

   What's your last name?

   How do you spell that?

4. Play the part of Student A. Walk around the classroom. Stop at the desk of an above-level student. Ask him or her to play the part of Student B. Then model the conversation:

   A: *What's your first name?*

   B: (Says his or her first name)

   A: *How do you spell that?*

   B: (Spells his or her first name)

   Write Student B's first name on the board.

5. Continue to model the activity:

   A: *What's your last name?*

   B: (Says his or her last name)

   A: *How do you spell that?*

   B: (Spells his or her last name)

   Write Student B's last name on the board.

6. Continue to play the role of Student A. Walk around the classroom. Stop at the desk of another above-level student. Ask him or her to play the part of Student C. Ask Student C for his or her first and last names and ask him or her to spell them. Write Student C's first and last names on the board.

7. Circulate during the activity to help students ask the questions and each other's names. Make sure they are transcribing their classmates' names correctly.

   Note: Even if students recognize their classmates' names and know how to spell them, make sure they practice spelling the names in English.

Multilevel Options

Pre-level: If pre-level students have trouble understanding the names as their classmates spell them, allow them to ask: *Can you write that for me, please?*

Above-level: Challenge above-level students to do the activity without looking at the board.

Extension

After the class has finished the activity, have students line up in alphabetical order according to their last names.

Survey: *How do you spell that?*

First Name	Last Name

Information Gap: *Who's that?*

Grouping	Pairs
Target Language	*Be:* affirmative, contractions, subject pronouns *she* and *he*
Materials	Activity Master 3
Class Time	20 minutes

Teacher Preparation

• Copy Activity Master 3, one for every two students.

• Cut each copy into three parts. Clip together the illustration, Information Card A, and Information Card B.

Procedure

1. Put students in like-ability pairs. Give a copy of Information Card A to Student A and a copy of Information Card B to Student B in each pair. Give each pair the illustration to share.

2. Hold up a copy of the illustration. Point to the question box at the bottom of the illustration. Explain that students are going to fill in the missing information in their information cards by asking each other: *Who's that? Where's _____ from? How do you spell that?*

3. On the board write: *Who's that?* and *How do you spell that?* Play the part of Student A. Call on an above-level student to play the part of Student B. Then model the activity:

    A: (Holds up the illustration and points to person number 1 in the illustration) *Who's that?*

    B: *That's Rosa.*

    A: *How do you spell that?*

    B: *R-O-S-A.*

    Instruct all Student As to write *Rosa* on the first line of their information cards.

4. Continue to model the activity. On the board write: *Where's _____ from?* and *How do you spell that?* Instruct Student B to continue the conversation:

    B: *Where's Rosa from?*

    A: *She's from Mexico.*

    B: *How do you spell that?*

    A: *M-E-X-I-C-O.*

    Instruct all Student Bs to write *Mexico* on the first line of their information cards.

5. To give students more support, write the model conversation on the board.

6. Have pairs continue the activity. Tell students that they should take turns asking the names and countries of the people on their cards.

7. Tell students not to show each other their information cards.

8. Circulate during the activity to help students with spelling and to make sure they do not show their partners their information cards until the end of the activity.

9. When pairs have filled in all the names and countries, have partners compare cards to check their information. The names and the countries on both cards should be the same.

Multilevel Options

Pre-level: Give pre-level students some of the names to write on their information cards so they have fewer questions to ask. For example, for Student As, add *Jefferson* to item 3, and for Student Bs, add *Mariam* to item 4.

Above-level: Have above-level students fold the question box below the illustration and form the questions on their own.

Extension

If some pairs finish before the rest of the class, have them write a list of their classmates and their countries. Tell students they have five minutes. Then see who has the longest list.

Information Gap: *Who's that?*

Who's that?   Where's _____ from?   How do you spell that?

Information Card A	Information Card B
1. Name: _____ Country: Mexico	1. Name: Rosa Country: _____
2. Name: Wen Country: _____	2. Name: _____ Country: China
3. Name: _____ Country: Brazil	3. Name: Jefferson Country: _____
4. Name: Mariam Country: _____	4. Name: _____ Country: Somalia
5. Name: _____ Country: India	5. Name: Talib Country: _____

Picture-based Story: *Kwan's First Day in English Class*

Grouping	Pairs and then whole class
Target Language	Identifying students, talking about school, questions
Materials	Activity Master 4
Class Time	25 minutes

Teacher Preparation

Copy Activity Master 4, one for each student.

Procedure

1. Give a copy of Activity Master 4 to each student.

2. Explain that students are going to write a story based on the picture.

3. Put students in cross-ability pairs to discuss the questions on Activity Master 4.

4. Have students report their ideas to the class. Make sure students understand the scene: The students are doing an activity. They're enjoying the activity, but Kwan thinks it is hard.

5. Ask the class: *What's the story?* Have the class develop a story line orally.

6. Have students dictate the story line. Listen to students' ideas, repeat the ideas while rephrasing them in correct English, and write them on the board.

7. Have students copy the story into their notebooks.

Multilevel Option

Above-level: After they copy the story, have above-level students write comprehension questions about the story to ask the class.

Variation

Write the class story on an overhead projector transparency. This way you can photocopy the story for the following class and have students reread the text in pairs.

Extension

After the class has finished the activity, erase words from the story and have students tell you the missing words.

Picture-based Story: *Kwan's First Day in English Class*

PAIRS: Talk about the picture.

• Where are the students?

• Is the class interesting?

• Are the students friendly?

• Is Kwan happy? What's the problem?

• What happens next?

CLASS: Tell the story to the teacher.

Board Game: *Getting to Know You*

Grouping	Groups of 4
Target Language	*Be:* affirmative and negative, contractions, questions
Materials	Activity Master 5, a coin, two markers for each group
Class Time	20 minutes

Teacher Preparation

Copy Activity Master 5, one for every four students.

Procedure

1. Put students in like-ability pairs. Each pair is a team. Put two teams together to play the game. Give each group of 4 a copy of Activity Master 5, a coin, and two markers.

2. Explain that students are going to play a board game. Here are the rules:

   • Pair 1 flips a coin to move. Heads means the team moves their marker ahead two squares; tails means the team moves their marker ahead one square.

   • Pair 1 moves the marker to a square. Student A reads the question aloud. Student B answers with true information. Pair 2 listens to make sure Pair 1's answer is correct.

   • If Pair 1's answer is correct, Pair 2 takes a turn.

   • If Pair 1's answer is incorrect, Pair 1 moves the marker back one square, and Pair 2 takes a turn.

   • If a pair lands on a square that already has a marker on it, the pair gets to move forward one square.

   • The first pair to reach FINISH wins.

3. Circulate during the activity to make sure students' answers are correct.

Extension

If some groups finish before the rest of the class, have each student write two sentences about his or her partner. For example:

He's José Orellana. He's from Colombia.

Board Game: *Getting to Know You*

START	**1** Who's here today? (Name three students.) →	**2** How's your English class? →	**3** Who's your English teacher? ↓
7 Where are you from? ↓	**6** How do you spell your last name? ←	**5** How do you spell your country's name? ←	**4** What's your last name? ←
8 Where are students in your class from? (Name three students and countries.) →	**9** Where's your teacher from? →	**10** What English class are you in? →	**11** How's your English teacher? ↓
FINISH	**14** How do you spell your first name? ←	**13** How are the students in your English class? ←	**12** Who's absent today? ←

Unit 2 • Lesson 3

Future 1 pages 30–31

Survey: *What do you do?*

Grouping	Whole-class mixer
Target Language	Jobs, *a/an, be*
Materials	Activity Master 6
Class Time	20 minutes

Teacher Preparation

Copy Activity Master 6, one for each student.

Procedure

1. Give a copy of Activity Master 6 to each student.

2. Explain that students are going to walk around the classroom to take a survey. Students will ask each other about their jobs and write the information in the chart on Activity Master 6. Tell students they will have 15 minutes for the activity.

3. Go over the word box on Activity Master 6 to make sure students are familiar with the jobs. Ask several students: *What do you do?* If students have jobs that are not in the box, write them on the board for reference.

4. Play the part of Student A. Walk around the classroom. Stop at the desk of an above-level student. Ask him or her to play the part of Student B. Then model the activity:

   A: *What do you do?*

   B: *I'm a/an _____.*

   A: *Oh, that's interesting.*

   Write Student B's job on the board.

5. Continue to model the activity:

   A: *How do you spell your name?*

   B: (Spells his or her name)

   Write Student B's name next to his or her job on the board.

6. Continue to play the role of Student A. Walk around the classroom. Stop at the desk of another above-level student. Ask him or her to play the part of Student C. Ask Student C what his or her job is, and ask him or her to spell his or her name. Write Student C's answers on the board.

7. Circulate during the activity to help students ask and answer the two questions. Students may also need help spelling and writing the names and the jobs.

Multilevel Options

Pre-level: During the activity, have pre-level students refer to the jobs on the board as well as in the word box on Activity Master 6.

Above-level: Tell above-level students to do the activity without looking at the word box.

Extension

After the class has finished the activity, have students look at the information in their surveys and write sentences about their classmates on the board. For example:

Lino is a cashier.

Alexi and Maria are nurses.

Survey: *What do you do?*

Name	Job

Jobs			
accountant	artist	cashier	child-care worker
cook	doctor	driver	electrician
gardener	homemaker	housekeeper	nurse
office assistant	painter	sales assistant	waiter

Tic-Tac-Toe: *Questions with* To Be

Grouping Groups of 4
Target Language *Be: yes/no* questions and short answers, jobs
Materials Activity Master 7
Class Time 20 minutes

Teacher Preparation

Copy Activity Master 7, one for every four students.

Procedure

1. Create a class fact list that students can refer to during the activity. Call on each student and ask: *What do you do?* On the board, write the student's name and occupation. For example:

   Paco—electrician

   Ming—child-care worker

2. Put students in like-ability pairs. Each pair is a team. Put two teams together to play the game. Give each group of 4 a copy of Activity Master 7.

3. Explain that students are going to play Tic-Tac-Toe with true questions and answers about their classmates' jobs. Students on each team will create a correct question that can be matched with a true answer in the grid. Here are the rules:

   • A student on Team A points to an answer in the grid (for example, *Yes, he is.*) and then asks a question (for example, *Is Paco an electrician?*) Since *Yes, he is* is the true answer, Team A marks an **X** over that answer in the grid.

   • Team B takes a turn by pointing to an answer and asking a question. If the question and answer are correct and true, Team B marks an **O** over the answer in the grid.

   • The first team to get three marks in a row—vertically, horizontally, or diagonally—wins.

4. Circulate during the activity to make sure that students' questions are grammatically correct and the answers are true.

5. Have teams play a second round.

Multilevel Option

Above-level: Have above-level students write the questions while they play the game.

Extension

If some groups finish before the rest of the class, have each student unscramble these job names:

   mmaeeorhk (homemaker)

   ncaoutncta (accountant)

   oock (cook)

   lessa sssaaittn (sales assistant)

Tic-Tac-Toe: *Questions with* To Be

Round 1

No, he isn't.	Yes, he is.	Yes, they are.
Yes, she is.	No, she isn't.	Yes, we are.
No, they aren't.	No, we aren't.	Yes, she is.

Round 2

Yes, we are.	No, she isn't.	No, they aren't.
No, we aren't.	Yes, they are.	No, he isn't.
Yes, she is.	Yes, he is.	No, we aren't.

Picture-based Story: *Job Skills*

Grouping	Pairs and then whole class
Target Language	Jobs, job skills
Materials	Activity Master 8
Class Time	25 minutes

Teacher Preparation

Copy Activity Master 8, one for each student.

Procedure

1. Give a copy of Activity Master 8 to each student.

2. Explain that students are going to write a story based on the picture.

3. Put students in cross-ability pairs to discuss the questions on Activity Master 8.

4. Have students report their ideas to the class. Make sure students understand the scene: Mr. Pierre is talking to a job counselor. They're talking about his job skills.

5. Ask the class: *What's the story?* Have the class develop a story line orally.

6. Have students dictate the story line. Listen to students' ideas, repeat the ideas while rephrasing them in correct English, and write them on the board.

7. Have students copy the story into their notebooks.

Multilevel Option

Above-level: After they copy the story, have above-level students write comprehension questions about the story to ask the class.

Variation

Write the class story on an overhead projector transparency. This way you can photocopy the story for the following class and have students reread the text in pairs.

Extension

After the class has finished the activity, erase words from the story and have students tell you the missing words.

Picture-based Story: *Job Skills*

PAIRS: Talk about the picture.

- Who is the job counselor?

- Why is Mr. Pierre in the job counselor's office?

- What are his job skills?

- What questions does the job counselor ask Mr. Pierre?

- What questions does Mr. Pierre ask the job counselor?

- What happens next?

CLASS: Tell the story to the teacher.

Unit 2 • Lesson 8

Find Someone Who: *Jobs and Workplaces*

Grouping	Whole-class mixer
Target Language	Jobs, workplaces
Materials	Activity Master 9
Class Time	20 minutes

Teacher Preparation

- Copy Activity Master 9, one for each student.

- Cut out the chart on each copy. Cut enough cards so that each student has an occupation.

Procedure

1. Give each student a copy of the chart and a card with an occupation. Give an above-level student the card with *cook* as the occupation. You'll need to call on the student when you model the activity in step 3 below.

2. Explain that students are going to pretend that the occupation on their card is their real-life occupation. Tell them that they will walk around the classroom. They will ask and answer *What do you do?* and *Where do you work?* in order to complete as many sentences in the chart as possible. Tell students they will have 15 minutes for the activity.

3. Write *What do you do? Where do you work?* on the board. Play the part of Student A. Walk around the classroom. Stop at the desk of the student you gave the card to. Have him or her play the part of Student B. Model the conversation:

   A: *What do you do?*

   B: *I'm a cook.*

   A: *Where do you work?*

   B: (Looks at chart and chooses correct workplace) *I work at a restaurant.*

   A: (Writes students name next to *works at a restaurant* in the chart)

4. To give students more support, write the model conversation on the board.

5. Circulate during the activity to help students formulate questions and answers correctly.

Multilevel Options

Pre-level: If pre-level students have difficulty writing their classmates' names, allow them to ask: *Can you write that for me please?* Also have pre-level students refer to the conversation on the board.

Above-level: Challenge above-level students to do the activity without looking at the board.

Extension

After the class has finished the activity, write the occupations on the board. Instruct students to match the occupations with the workplaces. Write their answers on the board. Tell students that some occupations might have more than one possible workplace. For example, a cashier could work at a restaurant or a store.

Variation

Have students do the activity in groups of 4. After five minutes, have students read aloud their sentences. The rest of the class listens and completes Activity Master 9.

Find Someone Who: *Jobs and Workplaces*

cook	nurse	carpenter	stock clerk	homemaker
doctor	waiter	sales assistant	teacher	caregiver
child-care worker	office assistant	accountant	assembly-line worker	cashier

Name	
	works at a restaurant.
	works at a home.
	works at a construction site.
	works at a store.
	works at an office.
	works at a nursing home.
	works at a school.
	works at a hospital.
	works at a factory.
	works at a child-care center.

Board Game: *Are you a student?*

Grouping	Groups of 4
Target Language	Jobs, *be:* affirmative and negative, contractions, questions
Materials	Activity Master 10, a coin, two markers for each group
Class Time	20 minutes

Teacher Preparation

Copy Activity Master 10, one for every four students.

Procedure

1. Put students in like-ability pairs. Each pair is a team. Put two teams together to play the game. Give each group of 4 a copy of Activity Master 10, a coin, and two markers.

2. Explain that students are going to play a board game. Here are the rules:

   • Pair 1 flips a coin to move. Heads means the team moves their marker ahead two squares; tails means the team moves their marker ahead one square.

   • Pair 1 moves the marker to a square. Student A reads the question aloud. Student B answers with true information. Pair 2 listens to make sure Pair 1's answer is correct.

   • If Pair 1's answer is correct, Pair 2 takes a turn.

   • If Pair 1's answer is incorrect, Pair 1 moves the marker back one square, and Pair 2 takes a turn.

   • If a pair lands on a square that already has a marker on it, the pair gets to move forward one square.

   • The first pair to reach FINISH wins.

3. Circulate during the activity to make sure students' answers are correct.

Extension

If some groups finish before the rest of the class, have each student write three true sentences about his or her partner. For example:

> Mark is an accountant.
> He works at an office.
> He's good with numbers.

Board Game: *Are you a student?*

START	**1** What do you do? →	**2** Where do you work? →	**3** Some people need uniforms at work. Do you? ↓
7 What's your area code? ↓	**6** Are you organized? ←	**5** What's your phone number? ←	**4** Where does an accountant work? ←
8 Are you a student? →	**9** Where does an assembly-line worker work? →	**10** Are you good with numbers? →	**11** Where does a carpenter work? ↓
FINISH	**14** Are you good with people? ←	**13** Are you a homemaker? ←	**12** Where does a sales assistant work? ←

Build a Sentence: *Classroom Instructions*

Grouping Pairs
Target Language Things in the classroom, classroom instructions
Materials Activity Master 11
Class Time 20 minutes

Teacher Preparation

- Copy Activity Master 11, one for each pair of students.

- Cut each copy into 20 cards. The white cards are sentence beginnings, and the gray cards are sentence endings.

- Clip each set of cards together.

Procedure

1. Put students in like-ability pairs. Give each pair a set of cards.

2. Tell Student A to shuffle the white cards and Student B to shuffle the gray cards. Have each student put their cards faceup on their desks.

3. Explain that students are going to work together to make ten correct sentences with the cards. Tell students that the white cards are sentence beginnings and the gray cards are sentence endings.

4. Model the activity. Assemble a white card and a gray card into a correct sentence and read it aloud. *Don't look at your books.*

5. Write the sentence on the board. Tell students to assemble the sentence with their cards.

6. Tell students to continue to assemble correct sentences.

7. Circulate during the activity to make sure students' matched sentences are correct.

Multilevel Option

Pre-level: Follow the dark horizontal line on Activity Master 11 to separate the set into halves. Give pre-level students only the first ten cards so that they have fewer choices to consider as they match the cards. When they finish the first half of the cards, give them the second half.

Extension

If some pairs complete the activity before the rest of the class, have partners take turns picking up a card and saying a sentence with the words. The other partner writes the sentence down and corrects it if necessary.

Variation

Mixer: Use one copy of Activity Master 11. Give each student a card at random. Have students walk around the classroom, each student continuously saying his or her half of the sentence until he or she finds the matching half. If there are more than 20 students, use two copies of Activity Master 11.

Answer Key
Don't look at your books.
Take out a piece of paper.
Use a pencil. Don't use a pen.
Write your name on the paper.
Open your books to page 6.
Listen to your teacher.
Don't eat in class.
Try to come on time.
Put away your notebooks.
Bring your dictionary to class.

Build a Sentence: *Classroom Instructions*

Don't look	at your books.
Take out a	piece of paper.
Use a	pencil. Don't use a pen.
Write your	name on the paper.
Open your	books to page 6.
Listen	to your teacher.
Don't eat	in class.
Try to	come on time.
Put away	your notebooks.
Bring your	dictionary to class.

Picture-based Story: *Trouble with Homework*

Grouping	Pairs and then whole class
Target Language	Study habits
Materials	Activity Master 12
Class Time	25 minutes

Teacher Preparation

Copy Activity Master 12, one for each student.

Procedure

1. Give a copy of Activity Master 12 to each student.

2. Explain that students are going to write a story based on the picture.

3. Put students in cross-ability pairs to discuss the questions on Activity Master 12.

4. Have students report their ideas to the class. Make sure students understand the scene: Katya needs help. She has terrible study habits.

5. Ask the class: *What's the story?* Have the class develop a story line orally.

6. Have students dictate the story line. Listen to students' ideas, repeat the ideas while rephrasing them in correct English, and write them on the board.

7. Have students copy the story into their notebooks.

Multilevel Option

Above-level: After they copy the story, have above-level students write comprehension questions about the story to ask the class.

Variations

Variation 1: Write the class story on an overhead projector transparency. This way you can photocopy the story for the following class and have students reread the text in pairs.

Variation 2: Have students write a letter to Katya and tell her how to be a better student.

Extension

After the class has finished the activity, erase words from the story and have students tell you the missing words.

Picture-based Story: *Trouble with Homework*

PAIRS: Talk about the picture.

• What is Katya doing?

• Is Katya a good student? Why or why not?

• How can Katya be a better student?

• What happens in her next class?

CLASS: Tell the story to the teacher.

Unit 3 • Lesson 6

Question and Answer Game: *What's that called in English?*

Grouping	Three teams
Target Language	*This, that, these, those:* questions and answers
Materials	Activity Master 13, a watch with a second hand
Class Time	20 minutes

Teacher Preparation

- Copy Activity Master 13, one for the whole class.

- Cut the copy into 24 cards.

- Read the cards and discard any cards that name objects that are not in your classroom.

Procedure

1. Divide the class into three cross-ability teams, A, B, and C.

2. Keep all the cards in a deck at the front of the class. Make sure the card with *a desk* is the first card of the deck. You will need it for the model activity in Step 6.

3. Explain that teams compete against each other. One member of Team A comes to the front of the room and chooses the top card from the deck. That student reads the card silently and finds the object pictured on the card in the classroom. He or she points to the object and asks his or her teammates what the object is.

4. Write Team A, Team B, and Team C on the board to keep score.

5. Write these questions on the board:

   What's that?

   What are those?

6. Play the part of Team A, Student A. Call on an above-level student to play the part of Team A, Student B. Then model the activity:

   A: (Picks a card: *a desk*. Points to a desk.) *What's that?*
   B: *That's a desk.*
   A: *Right!* (Writes *a desk* on the board)
   A player on Team B goes next.

Note: The question must be grammatically correct, and the answer must agree with the singular or plural question. For example, to answer the question *What are those?* a student must say *pens. A pen* is not an acceptable response. When either the question or the answer is not correct, the player returns the card to the bottom of the deck and the next team takes a turn.

7. Have teams take turns picking a card, asking questions, and identifying the classroom objects. Act as timekeeper or choose a student to keep time for each round and limit each question-and-answer exchange to ten seconds. Make sure all students participate.

Multilevel Option

Pre-level: To allow pre-level students to participate more fully, have teams pick cards and make notes before the game begins.

Variation

Make one copy of Activity Master 13 for every four students. Have students play the game with two teams of two students each. Circulate to make sure students' questions and answers are correct.

Extension

After the class has finished the activity, hand out the word cards to students and have them tape the cards on the corresponding objects around the classroom.

Question and Answer Game: *What's that called in English?*

a desk	pencils	a backpack
chairs	a board	an eraser
a folder	markers	books
a dictionary	pens	a three-ring binder
a piece of paper	notebooks	a cell phone
a piece of chalk	a map	a computer
CDs	a mouse	a monitor
a chart	a keyboard	a picture

School Treasure Hunt: *Where is it?*

Grouping	Whole-class mixer
Target Language	Places at school
Materials	Activity Master 14
Class Time	20 minutes

Teacher Preparation

• Before copying Activity Master 14, read the lists of places and people at school. You may want to tape over some words and substitute other places. Add three rooms in your school to the chart.

• Copy Activity Master 14, one for each student.

Procedure

1. Give a copy of Activity Master 14 to each student.

2. Explain that students are going to walk around the classroom. They will ask and answer *Where's the* _____? in order to complete the chart on Activity Master 14. Tell students they will have 15 minutes for the activity.

3. Walk around the classroom. Stop at the desk of an above-level student. Then model the conversation:

   A: *Excuse me. Where's the cafeteria?*

   B: (Answers question)

   A: *Thank you.* (Writes the location in chart on Activity Master 14)

4. To give students more support, write the model conversation on the board.

5. Circulate during the activity to make sure students are asking and answering questions correctly.

Multilevel Options

Pre-level and above-level: Have pre-level students ask the questions and above-level students answer the questions.

Variation

In groups of three, have students walk around the school building and ask people where the rooms are.

Extension

After the class has finished the activity, have students draw a map of their school. Have them include the elevators, stairways, classrooms, library, offices, and cafeteria. Have pairs share their maps.

School Treasure Hunt: *Where is it?*

Places at School	Where is it?
computer lab	
main office	
library	
cafeteria	
principal's office	
elevator	
restroom	

Board Game: *At School*

Grouping	Groups of 4
Target Language	Things in the classroom, numbers 10–100, people and places at school, study habits
Materials	Activity Master 15, a coin, two markers for each group
Class Time	20 minutes

Teacher Preparation

Copy Activity Master 15, one for every four students.

Procedure

1. Put students in like-ability pairs. Each pair is a team. Put two teams together to play the game. Give each group of 4 a copy of Activity Master 15, a coin, and two markers.

2. Explain that students are going to play a board game. Here are the rules:

   • Pair 1 flips a coin to move. Heads means the team moves their marker ahead two squares; tails means the team moves their marker ahead one square.

   • Pair 1 moves the marker to a square. Student A reads the prompt aloud. Student B responds to it. Pair 2 listens to make sure Pair 1's answer is correct.

   • If Pair 1's answer is correct, Pair 2 takes a turn.

   • If Pair 1's answer is incorrect, Pair 1 moves the marker back one square, and Pair 2 takes a turn.

   • If a pair lands on a square that already has a marker on it, the pair gets to move forward one square.

   • The first pair to reach FINISH wins.

3. Circulate during the activity to make sure students' answers are correct.

Extension

If some groups finish before the rest of the class, have each student write a list of all the objects he or she sees in the classroom. Then have pairs compare their lists.

Answer Key

2. 37, 81, 23
3. It's across from Room 229. OR It's next to the stairs.
5. False
6. False
11. 78, 63, 49
13. 52, 26, 94
15. It's next to Room 229. OR It's next to the elevator. OR It's across from the stairs.

Board Game: *At School*

START / FINISH	1 Where's the library in your school? →	2 Write these numbers: thirty-seven, eighty-one, twenty-three. →	3 Look at the picture. Where's the computer lab? →	4 Name eight things in your classroom. ↓
15 Look at the picture. Where's Room 230? ↑				5 Look at the picture. The stairs are next to the restroom. True or false? ↓
14 Write your first and last names. Circle your first name. Underline your last name. ↑				6 Look at the picture. The cafeteria is across from the office. True or false? ↓
13 Write these numbers: fifty-two, twenty-six, ninety-four. ↑				7 Where's the cafeteria in your school? ↓
12 Name four people who work in your school. ↑	11 Write these numbers: seventy-eight, sixty-three, forty-nine. ←	10 Answer this question: Is this a test? ←	9 What room number is your classroom? ←	8 What are two good study habits? ←

Information Gap: *Who's Pam?*

Grouping Pairs
Target Language Family members, possessive nouns, questions with *Who*
Materials Activity Master 16
Class 20 minutes

Teacher Preparation

- Copy Activity Master 16, one for each pair of students.

- Cut out the two family trees. Clip together each set of family trees A and B.

Procedure

1. Put students in like-ability pairs. Give a copy of Family Tree A to Student A and a copy of Family Tree B to Student B.

2. Hold up a copy of both family trees. Point to the question at the bottom of each family tree. Explain that students are going to fill in the missing information in their family trees by asking each other: *Who's _____?*

3. Play the part of Student A. Call on an above-level student to play the part of Student B. Then model the activity:

   A: *Who's Pam?*

   B: *Sam's wife.*

   Instruct all Student As to write the name *Pam* in the correct place on their family tree.

   Note: If students ask about the relationship between Pam and Ann, for example, explain that people married into a family are called in-laws. Pam is Ann's daughter-in-law, and Ann is Pam's mother-in-law.

4. Continue to model the activity. Instruct Student B to continue the conversation:

   B: *Who's Lisa?*

   A: *Greg's wife.*

   Instruct all Student Bs to write *Lisa* in the correct place on their family tree.

Note: Tell students that more than one answer is possible. For example, the answer to *Who's Lisa?* could also be *Ann's daughter*.

4. To give students more support, write the model questions and answers on the board.

5. Have pairs continue the activity. Partners should take turns asking about the people missing from their family trees.

6. Tell students not to show each other their family trees.

7. Circulate during the activity to help students with pronunciation and to make sure they do not show their partners their family trees until the end of the activity.

8. When pairs have filled in all the names, have them compare family trees to check their information. The names on both family trees should be the same.

Multilevel Option

Pre-level: Give pre-level students some of the names to write in their family trees so they have fewer questions to ask and more information to support their answers. For example, for Student As, add *Bob* (Ann's husband), and for Student Bs, add *Tim* (Beth's husband).

Extension

If some pairs finish before the rest of the class, have each student write sentences describing a family member in the Smith family. For example:

> Beth is Bob and Ann's daughter.
>
> Beth is Sam and Lisa's sister. Beth is Amy and Don's mother.

Then have pairs compare their lists.

Information Gap: *Who's Pam?*

Family Tree A

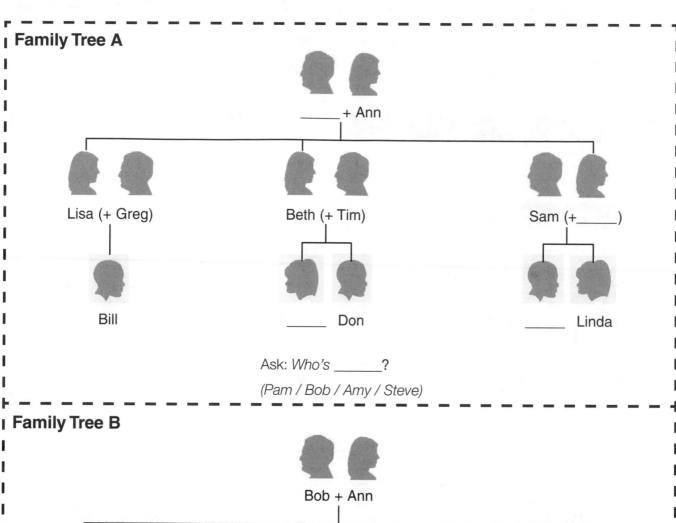

_____ + Ann

Lisa (+ Greg)   Beth (+ Tim)   Sam (+_____)

Bill   _____ Don   _____ Linda

Ask: *Who's _____?*

(Pam / Bob / Amy / Steve)

Family Tree B

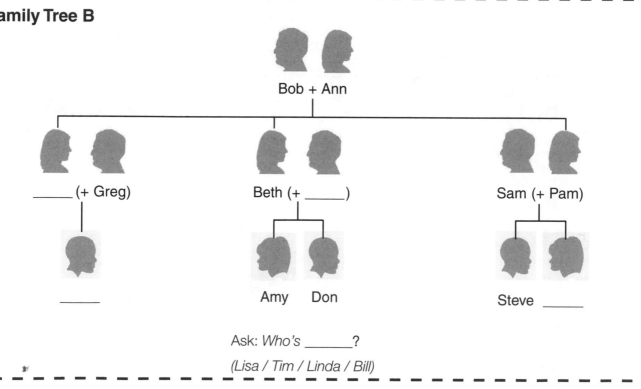

Bob + Ann

_____ (+ Greg)   Beth (+ _____)   Sam (+ Pam)

_____   Amy   Don   Steve _____

Ask: *Who's _____?*

(Lisa / Tim / Linda / Bill)

Picture-based Story: *The Pinters: A Blended Family*

Grouping	Pairs and then whole class
Target Language	Family members, possessive adjectives, describing people
Materials	Activity Master 17
Class Time	25 minutes

Teacher Preparation

Copy Activity Master 17, one for each student.

Procedure

1. Give each student a copy of Activity Master 17.

2. Explain that students are going to write a story based on the picture.

3. Put students in cross-ability pairs to discuss the questions on Activity Master 17.

4. Have students report their ideas to the class. Make sure students understand the scene: Mr. and Mrs. Pinter just got married. The Pinters are now a blended family.

5. Ask the class: *What's the story?* Have the class develop a story line orally.

6. Have students dictate the story line. Listen to students' ideas, repeat the ideas while rephrasing them in correct English, and write them on the board.

7. Have students copy the story into their notebooks.

Multilevel Option

Above-level: After they copy the story, have above-level students write comprehension questions about the story to ask the class.

Variation

Write the class story on an overhead projector transparency. This way you can photocopy the story for the following class and have students reread the text in pairs.

Extension

After the class has finished the activity, erase words from the story and have students tell you the missing words.

Picture-based Story: *The Pinters: A Blended Family*

PAIRS: Talk about the picture.

- Who is Mrs. Pinter? Who is Mr. Pinter?
- Who does the girl look like?
- Who do the boys look like?
- Are the mother and father happy?
- Are the children happy?
- What happens next?

CLASS: Tell the story to the teacher.

Unit 4 • Lesson 6

Build a Sentence: *Describing People*

Grouping Pairs
Target Language Descriptions with *be* and *have*
Materials Activity Master 18
Class Time 15 minutes

Teacher Preparation

• Copy Activity Master 18, one for each pair of students.

• Cut each Activity Master into 18 cards. The top nine word cards are for sentences with *have*. The bottom nine word cards are for sentences with *be*. Follow the dark horizontal line on Activity Master 18 to separate the set into halves.

• Clip each set of cards together.

Procedure

1. Put students in cross-ability pairs. Give Student A the cards for *have* sentences. Give Student B the cards for *be* sentences.

2. Tell each pair to shuffle their cards. Have students put their cards faceup on their desks.

3. Explain that students are going to work together to assemble as many sentences as possible. Have the pre-level student in each pair copy the sentences into a notebook. Tell students they will have ten minutes for the activity.

4. Model the activity. Assemble three cards into a sentence and read it aloud: *I have short hair.*

   S: B Write sent. on board.

5. Write the sentence on the board. Tell students to assemble the sentence with their cards.

6. Tell students to continue to assemble correct sentences.

7. Circulate during the activity to make sure students' matched sentences are correct.

Multilevel Option

Pre-level: Give pre-level students only the first nine cards so they can focus on making sentences with *have*. When students finish, give them the second nine so they can focus on making sentences with *be*.

Extension

If some pairs complete the activity within ten minutes, have students take turns picking up a card and saying a sentence with the word. The partner writes the sentence down and corrects it if necessary.

Answer Key

Possible sentences:

I have short hair.	He's average height.
I have a beard.	He's short.
I'm average height.	He's tall.
I'm short.	She has short hair.
I'm tall.	She's tall.
We're average height.	She's average height.
We're short.	She's short.
We're tall.	They have short hair.
You're tall.	They have beards.
You're average height.	They're tall.
You're short.	They're average height.
He has short hair.	They're short.
He has a beard.	

Build a Sentence: *Describing People*

I	have	short hair.
They	has	a beard.
He	She	beards.
I'm	You're	We're
They're	He's	She's
short.	average height.	tall.

Picture Match: *How old is she?*

Grouping Whole-class mixer
Target Language Describing people, ages, grades in school
Materials Activity Master 19
Class Time 20 minutes

Teacher Preparation

- Copy Activity Master 19. Make enough copies so there will be one card for each student, plus extra cards for students who finish early.

- Cut each copy into four cards.

Procedure

1. Give each student a card at random. Have students look at the picture of the woman and read her age and grade.

2. Explain that students are going to walk around the classroom and ask and answer questions in order to find a matching card. Tell students not to show their cards to anyone. They will have 15 minutes for the activity.

3. Write the following questions on the board:

   Is she tall / short / thin / heavy?

   How old is she?

   What grade is she in?

4. Have students look at the pictures and read the information.

5. Play the part of Student A. Look at your card. Walk around the classroom. Stop at the desk of an above-level student. Ask him or her to play the part of Student B. Ask the questions on the board. Continue to call on above-level students until you get a match.

6. To give students more support, write this model conversation on the board:

   A: Is she tall?

   B: Yes, she is.

   A: How old is she?

   B: She's 18.

   A: Oh, she's 17 in my picture.

   Note: Remind students that they should continue to question students until they find a match.

7. Circulate during the activity to make sure students are not showing anyone their cards.

8. When students find a match, give each another card to continue the game.

Multilevel Options

Pre-level: During the activity, allow pre-level students to refer to the questions on the board.

Above-level: Tell above-level students to do the activity without looking at the questions on the board.

Extension

After the class has finished the activity, have students sit with a partner who has a different card. Have pairs write sentences about everything that is the same on their two cards. For example:

   They are both thin.

   They both have long hair.

Picture Match: *How old is she?*

Age: 18

Grade: Twelfth

Age: 17

Grade: Eleventh

Age: 16

Grade: Eleventh

Age: 17

Grade: Twelfth

Board Game: *The Becker Family*

Grouping Groups of 4
Target Language Family members, dates of birth
Materials Activity Master 20, a coin, two markers for each group
Class Time 20 minutes

Teacher Preparation

Copy Activity Master 20, one for every four students.

Procedure

1. Put students in like-ability pairs. Each pair is a team. Put two teams together to play the game. Give each group of 4 a copy of Activity Master 20, a coin, and two markers.

2. Explain that students are going to play a board game. Here are the rules:

   • Pair 1 flips a coin to move. Heads means the team moves their marker ahead two squares; tails means the team moves their marker ahead one square.

   • Pair 1 moves the marker to a square. Student A reads the question aloud. Student B answers with true information. Pair 2 listens to make sure Pair 1's answer is correct.

   • If Pair 1's answer is correct, Pair 2 takes a turn.

   • If Pair 1's answer is incorrect, Pair 1 moves the marker back one square, and Pair 2 takes a turn.

   • If a pair lands on a square that already has a marker on it, the pair gets to move forward one square.

   • The first pair to reach FINISH wins.

3. Circulate during the activity to make sure students' answers are correct.

Extension

If some groups finish before the rest of the class, have them write three more questions about the Becker family. Then have them take turns asking and answering questions.

Answer Key

1. Yes, she does.
2. No, he doesn't.
3. September twenty-first, nineteen seventy-five
4. *Answer depends on the current year.*
5. Susan
6. Jane
7. John
8. *Answer depends on the current year.*
9. No, he doesn't.
10. August seventh, nineteen seventy
11. Jane
12. John
13. Susan
14. Mike
15. Steve

Board Game: *The Becker Family*

START	1	2	3	4
FINISH	Does Susan look like her mother? →	Does Mike look like his father? →	What is Will's date of birth? (Say it in words.) →	How old is Steve? ↓

15

His father is Tom. Who is he?

↑

5

Who is John's daughter?

↓

The Becker Family

John 11/4/1945 + Jane 6/2/1950

Mike 4/11/1977   Will 9/21/1975   Susan 2/6/1973 + (Tom) 8/7/1970

Steve 7/8/2007

14

He has a beard. Who is he?

↑

6

She has short hair. Who is she?

↓

13

Her birthday is February 6. Who is she?

↑

7

His birthday is November 4. Who is he?

↓

12	11	10	9	8
His wife is Jane. Who is he? ↑	Who is Steve's grandmother? ←	What is Tom's date of birth? (Say it in words.) ←	Does Will look like his brother? ←	How old is Jane? ←

Survey: *What do you want for your birthday?*

Grouping	Whole-class mixer
Target Language	Simple present affirmative
Materials	Activity Master 21
Class Time	20 minutes

Teacher Preparation

Copy Activity Master 21, one for each student.

Procedure

1. Give a copy of Activity Master 21 to each student.

2. Explain that students are going to walk around the classroom to take a survey. Students will ask each other what they want for their next birthday and write the information in the chart on Activity Master 21. Tell students they will have 15 minutes for the activity.

3. Brainstorm items that students would like for their next birthday. Write their ideas on the board. Students may refer to this list during the activity.

4. Play the part of Student A. Walk around the classroom. Stop at the desk of an above-level student. Ask him or her to play the part of Student B. Then model the conversation:

   A: *What do you want for your next birthday?*

   B: (Tells Student A what he or she wants for his or her next birthday)

   A: *How do you spell that?*

   B: (Spells name of gift)

   Write Student B's name and his or her answer on the board.

5. Continue to play the role of Student A. Walk around the classroom. Stop at the desk of another above-level student. Ask him or her to play the part of Student C. Ask Student C the questions you asked Student B. Write Student C's answers on the board.

6. Circulate during the activity to help students spell new words. Students will probably mention non-clothing items, too.

7. After 15 minutes, ask students to sit down and tell the class about what they learned. For example: *Marcel wants a new watch. Maria wants a big party.*

Multilevel Options

Pre-level: During the activity, have pre-level students refer to the words on the board for ideas and spelling support.

Above-level: Have above-level students do the activity without looking at the words on the board.

Extension

After the class has finished the activity, have students write sentences based on their information in their charts. For example:

Carlos wants a new wallet.

Have students submit their sentences to you for feedback.

Survey: *What do you want for your birthday?*

Name	Birthday Gift

Information Gap: *How much?*

Grouping	Pairs
Target Language	Reading receipts, *How much?*
Materials	Activity Master 22
Class Time	20 minutes

Teacher Preparation

- Copy Activity Master 22, one for every two students.

- Cut out both receipts. Clip together each set of receipts A and B.

Procedure

1. Put students in like-ability pairs. Give a copy of Receipt A to Student A and a copy of Receipt B to Student B in each pair.

2. Hold up a copy of each receipt. Point to the question box next to each receipt. Explain that students are going to fill in the missing information on their receipts by asking each other questions beginning with *How much . . .*

3. On the board write *How much _____?* Play the part of Student A. Call on an above-level student to play the part of Student B. Then model the activity:

    A: *How much is the T-shirt?*

    B: *Ten dollars and twenty-five cents.*

    Instruct all Student As to write $10.25 on their receipts.

4. Continue to model the activity. Instruct Student B to continue the conversation:

    B: *How much is the sweater?*

    A: *Twenty-four dollars and fifty cents.*

    Instruct all Student Bs to write $24.50 on their receipts.

5. To give students more support, write the model conversation on the board.

6. Have pairs continue the activity. Partners should take turns asking about the missing amounts on their receipts and filling in the information.

7. Tell students not to show each other their receipts.

8. Circulate during the activity to help with question formation and to make sure students do not show their partners their receipts until the end of the activity.

9. When pairs have filled in all the blanks, have them compare receipts to check their information. The amounts on both receipts should be the same.

Multilevel Options

Pre-level: During the activity, have pre-level students refer to the questions in the question box on Activity Master 22.

Above-level: Have above-level students fold the question box under the receipt and form the questions on their own.

Extension

Write the following questions on the board:

> What's the name of the store?
>
> What's the date on the receipt?
>
> How much are the items <u>before</u> tax?
>
> How much are the items <u>after</u> tax?

After the class has finished the activity, have students work with a partner to answer the questions.

Information Gap: *How much?*

Receipt A

Real World Clothes
Falmouth Mall
207-555-9265

09-05-09		10:38 A.M.

MEN'S DEPARTMENT

T-SHIRT	1	_____
JEANS	1	_____
SWEATER	1	24.50
SHOES	1	_____
PANTS	1	45.00
Wallet	1	29.95
SUBTOTAL		209.57
TAX 5%		_____
TOTAL		220.05
CASH		221.00
CHANGE DUE		.95

Thank you! Please come again!

How much is the T-shirt?
How much are the jeans?
How much are the shoes?
How much is the tax?

Receipt B

Real World Clothes
Falmouth Mall
207-555-9265

09-05-09		10:38 A.M.

MEN'S DEPARTMENT

T-SHIRT	1	10.25
JEANS	1	39.88
SWEATER	1	_____
SHOES	1	59.99
PANTS	1	_____
Wallet	1	_____
SUBTOTAL		209.57
TAX 5%		10.48
TOTAL		220.05
CASH		221.00
CHANGE DUE		_____

Thank you! Please come again!

How much is the sweater?
How much are the pants?
How much is the wallet?
How much is the change?

Unit 5 • Lesson 6

Future 1 pages 96–97

Clothes Match: *Do you have a yellow sweater?*

Grouping	Whole-class mixer
Target Language	Clothes, sizes, prices, simple present: *yes/no* questions and short answers
Materials	Activity Master 23
Class Time	20 minutes

Teacher Preparation

• Copy Activity Master 23. Make enough copies so there will be one card for each student.

• Cut each copy into 20 cards.

Procedure

1. Give each student a card at random. Have students read the information on their cards.

2. Explain that students are going to walk around the classroom. They will ask and answer questions in order to find a matching card. Tell students not to show their cards to anyone. They will have 15 minutes for the activity.

3. Write the following questions on the board:

   Do you have a (color) sweater in a (size) ?

   How much is it?

4. Play the part of Student A. Read your card. Walk around the classroom. Stop at the desk of an above-level student. Ask him or her to play the part of Student B. Ask the questions on the board. Continue to call on above-level students until you get a match.

5. To give students more support, write this model conversation on the board:

   A: *Do you have a yellow sweater in a large?*

   B: *Yes, I do.*

   A: *How much is it?*

   B: *Sixty dollars.*

   A: *Oh. This sweater is sixteen dollars.*

   Note: Remind students that they should continue to question students until they find a match.

6. Circulate during the activity to make sure students are not showing anyone their cards and are clearly pronouncing the prices. When students find a match, give each another card to continue the game.

Multilevel Options

Pre-level: During the activity, allow pre-level students to refer to the questions on the board.

Above-level: Tell above-level students to do the activity without looking at the questions on the board.

Extension

If some students find their match(es) before the rest of the class, have them sit down and write a description of the clothing items on the cards. Students should write complete sentences. For example:

   It's a yellow sweater.

   It's a size large.

   It costs sixteen dollars.

46 Future 1 Multilevel Communicative Activities

Clothes Match: *Do you have a yellow sweater?*

A sweater Color: Yellow Size: L Price: $16.00	A sweater Color: Yellow Size: L Price: $16.00
A sweater Color: Yellow Size: L Price: $60.00	A sweater Color: Yellow Size: L Price: $60.00
A sweater Color: Yellow Size: XL Price: $17.00	A sweater Color: Yellow Size: XL Price: $17.00
A sweater Color: Yellow Size: XL Price: $70.00	A sweater Color: Yellow Size: XL Price: $70.00
A sweater Color: Red Size: S Price: $18.00	A sweater Color: Red Size: S Price: $18.00
A sweater Color: Red Size: S Price: $80.00	A sweater Color: Red Size: S Price: $80.00
A sweater Color: Black Size: XS Price: $19.00	A sweater Color: Black Size: XS Price: $19.00
A sweater Color: Black Size: XS Price: $90.00	A sweater Color: Black Size: XS Price: $90.00
A sweater Color: Black Size: M Price: $14.00	A sweater Color: Black Size: M Price: $14.00
A sweater Color: Black Size: M Price: $40.00	A sweater Color: Black Size: M Price: $40.00

Unit 5 • Lesson 9

Future 1 page 102

Picture-based Story: *I need to return this jacket.*

Grouping Pairs and then whole class
Target Language Returning something to a store
Materials Activity Master 24
Class Time 25 minutes

Teacher Preparation

Copy Activity Master 24, one for each student.

Procedure

1. Give a copy of Activity Master 24 to each student.

2. Explain that students are going to write a story based on the picture.

3. Put students in cross-ability pairs to discuss the questions on Activity Master 24.

4. Have students report their ideas to the class. Make sure students understand the scene: Tamara is returning a jacket to the store. The zipper is broken. She has a receipt.

5. Ask the class: *What's the story?* Have the class develop a story line orally.

6. Have students dictate the story line. Listen to students' ideas, repeat the ideas while rephrasing them in correct English, and write them on the board.

7. Have students copy the story into their notebooks.

Multilevel Option

Above-level: After they copy the story, have above-level students write comprehension questions about the story to ask the class.

Variation

Write the class story on an overhead projector transparency. This way you can photocopy the story for the following class and have students reread the text in pairs.

Extension

After the class has finished the activity, erase words from the story and have students tell you the missing words.

Picture-based Story: *I need to return this jacket.*

PAIRS: Talk about the picture.

• Where is Tamara?

• What is she doing? Why?

• What happens next?

CLASS: Tell the story to the teacher.

Board Game: *Clothes*

Grouping	Groups of 4
Target Language	Clothes, colors, simple present *yes/no* questions and short answers
Materials	Activity Master 25, a coin, and two markers for each group
Class Time	20 minutes

Teacher Preparation

Copy Activity Master 25, one for every four students.

Procedure

1. Put students in like-ability pairs. Each pair is a team. Put two teams together to play the game. Give each group of 4 a copy of Activity Master 25, a coin, and two markers.

2. Explain that students are going to play a board game. Here are the rules:

   • Pair 1 flips a coin to move. Heads means the team moves their marker ahead two squares; tails means the team moves their marker ahead one square.

   • Pair 1 moves the marker to a square. Student A reads the prompt aloud. Student B answers with true information. Pair 2 listens to make sure Pair 1's answer is correct.

   • If Pair 1's answer is correct, Pair 2 takes a turn.

   • If Pair 1's answer is incorrect, Pair 1 moves the marker back one square, and Pair 2 takes a turn.

   • If a pair lands on a square that already has a marker on it, the pair gets to move forward one square.

   • The first pair to reach FINISH wins.

3. Circulate during the activity to make sure students' answers are correct.

Extension

If some groups finish before the rest of the class, have them write a list of the clothes and colors their classmates are wearing. For example:

black sneakers

blue jeans

a red T-shirt

Answer Key

1. extra small, small, medium, large, extra large

7. five dollars and twelve cents, twenty-three dollars and thirty-four cents, forty-seven dollars and sixty-one cents, eighty-four dollars and seventy-three cents

12. twelve dollars and ninety-nine cents, thirty-one dollars and twenty-five cents, ninety-eight dollars and fifty-six cents, one hundred-five dollars and ten cents

---

Board Game: *Clothes*

START	**1** Name these sizes: XS, S, M, L, XL. →	**2** What is your partner wearing? →	**3** Is your partner wearing a watch? ↓
7 Say these prices: $5.12, $23.34, $47.61, $84.73. ↓	**6** What colors is your teacher wearing? ←	**5** Finish the sentence: "I like the color _____." ←	**4** Look at your class-mates. Who's wearing white socks? ←
8 Look at your class-mates. Who's wearing sneakers? →	**9** What new clothes do you want? →	**10** Look at your class-mates. Who's wearing jeans? →	**11** Do you have a beige backpack? ↓
FINISH	**14** What colors are you wearing? ←	**13** Why do people return clothes? Give three reasons. ←	**12** Say these prices: $12.99, $31.25, $98.56, $105.10. ←

Drawing Game: *My Partner's Room*

Grouping Pairs
Target Language *There is/There are*, rooms of a house and objects in the rooms
Materials Activity Master 26
Class Time 25 minutes

Teacher Preparation

Copy Activity Master 26, one for each student.

Procedure

1. Put students in like-ability pairs. Give each student a copy of Activity Master 26.

2. Hold up Activity Master 26. Explain that students are going to draw a bedroom on the left side using the items in the box. Then they will describe the room to their partners, who will draw what they hear without seeing the original drawing.

3. On the board, write the words *door* and *window* and point to examples of each in your classroom. Then write the following words from Unit 3: *next to, across from, on the right, on the left*. Review their meanings if necessary. Walk to different locations in the classroom and ask: *Am I next to the windows? Am I across from the desk? Am I on the right? Am I on the left?*

4. Play the part of Student A. Call on an above-level student to play the part of Student B. Then model the activity. Following the drawing conventions given, draw a bedroom on Activity Master 26. Then outline a rectangle on the board and have Student B draw the room as you describe. For example:

   A: *There's a bed on the left.*

   B: *Here?* (Points to the left-hand wall)

   A: *Yes.*

   Student B copies the bed shape provided.

   Note: Students may ask their partners to confirm the placement of the items by pointing to the picture, like Student B does above.

5. Continue to model the activity:

   A: *There are two small tables. One is to the left of the bed, and one is to the right of the bed.*

   Student B copies the table shape and draws a small table on each side of the bed.

6. Give students five minutes to plan and fill in their own rooms. Tell students not to show their rooms to their partners.

7. Have students describe their rooms to their partners. They will have a total of 15 minutes.

8. Circulate during the activity to help students ask clarifying questions when the drawings don't match. For example: *Where's the chair? What about the bed?*

9. After pairs have drawn each other's rooms, have them compare their drawings to check their information. Although the furniture and other items may not be drawn in exactly the same way, their placement should be the same.

Extension

If some pairs finish before the rest of the class, have them write about their partner's room. For example:

> There's a bed on the left.

> There's a dresser across from the bed.

Multilevel Options

Pre-level: Allow pre-level students to look at and copy each other's drawings. Then have them work together to write sentences about each room.

Above-level: Suggest that above-level students brainstorm other items to add to their drawings, such as a TV or a desk.

Drawing Game: *My Partner's Room*

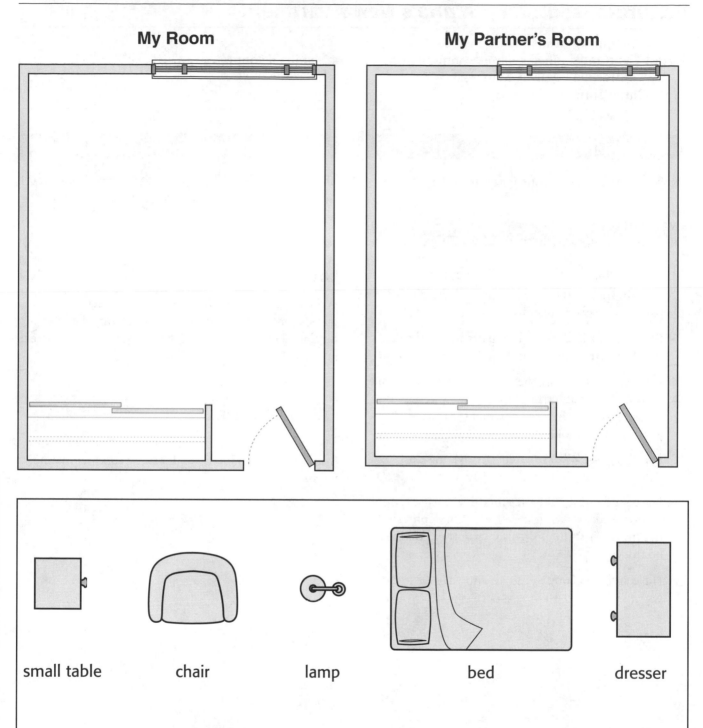

My Room

My Partner's Room

small table   chair   lamp   bed   dresser

Unit 6 • Lesson 4

Picture-based Story: *Maria's New Apartment*

Grouping Pairs and then whole class
Target Language Smoke alarms, rooms of a house and objects in the rooms
Materials Activity Master 27
Class Time 25 minutes

Teacher Preparation

Copy Activity Master 27, one for each student.

Procedure

1. Give a copy of Activity Master 27 to each student.

2. Explain that students are going to write a story based on the picture.

3. Put students in cross-ability pairs to discuss the questions on Activity Master 27.

4. Have students report their ideas to the class. Make sure students understand the scene: Maria and Carlos are in their new apartment. Maria is putting up a smoke alarm.

5. Ask the class: *What's the story?* Have the class develop a story line orally.

6. Have students dictate the story line. Listen to students' ideas, repeat the ideas while rephrasing them in correct English, and write them on the board.

7. Have students copy the story into their notebooks.

Multilevel Option

Above-level: After they copy the story, have above-level students write comprehension questions about the story to ask the class.

Variation

Write the class story on an overhead projector transparency. This way you can photocopy the story for the following class and have students reread the text in pairs.

Extension

After the class has finished the activity, erase words from the story and have students tell you the missing words.

Picture-based Story: *Maria's New Apartment*

PAIRS: Talk about the picture.

• Where is Maria?

• What is Maria doing? Why?

• What is Carlos doing? Why?

CLASS: Tell the story to the teacher.

Unit 6 • Lesson 6

Picture Match: *Is there a coffee table?*

Grouping	Whole-class mixer
Target Language	*Is there/Are there*, things in a room
Materials	Activity Master 28
Class Time	20 minutes

Teacher Preparation

- Copy Activity Master 28. Make enough copies so there will be one card for each student, plus extra cards for students who finish early.

- Cut each copy into six cards.

Procedure

1. Give one card to each student at random. Have students look at the picture of the living room on the card.

2. Explain that students are going to walk around the classroom. They will ask and answer questions in order to find a matching card. Tell students not to show their cards to anyone. They will have 15 minutes for the activity.

3. Write the following questions on the board:

   Is there a _____?
   Are there _____?

4. Have students look at the pictures and identify the objects: sofa, chair, coffee table, tables, floor lamp, table lamps, closet.

5. Play the part of Student A. Look at your card. Walk around the classroom. Ask an above-level student to play the part of Student B. Ask the questions on the board. Continue to call on above-level students until you get a match.

6. To give students more support, write this model conversation on the board:

   A: Is there a coffee table?

   B: Yes, there is.

   A: Are there table lamps?

   B: No, there aren't.

   A: Oh, my living room has table lamps.

   Note: Remind students that they should continue to question students until they find a match.

7. Circulate during the activity to make sure students are not showing anyone their cards and they are forming correct sentences.

8. When students find a match, give each another card to continue the activity.

Multilevel Options

Pre-level: During the activity, allow pre-level students to refer to the questions and conversation on the board.

Above-level: Tell above-level students to do the activity without looking at the board.

Extension

After the class has finished the activity, have students sit with a partner who has a different card. Have pairs talk about how their pictures are different. For example:

   A: *In my living room, there's no coffee table.*

   B: *In my living room, there are no table lamps.*

Picture Match: *Is there a coffee table?*

Question and Answer Game: *How do I get there?*

Grouping	Pairs
Target Language	Prepositions, giving directions
Materials	Activity Master 29
Class Time	20 minutes

Teacher Preparation

• Copy Activity Master 29, one for every two students.

• Cut each copy into 13 parts—the map and 12 cards. Clip each set together.

Procedure

1. Put students in like-ability pairs. Give each pair a map and a set of cards.

2. Explain that students are going to ask for and give directions. They will use the map to give each other directions to destinations written on the cards. Tell students they will have 15 minutes to do the activity.

3. Have students look at the map and identify the names of the businesses and the streets. Also have them locate the phrase *You are here* on the map.

4. Play the part of Student A. Call on an above-level student to play the part of Student B. Then model the activity. For this model, be sure to place the Central Bank card at the top of the pile. This is the card you will use in the model conversation below:

   A: (Picks a card: Central Bank) *How do I get to Central Bank from here?*

   B: *Go west on Second Avenue to the light. Turn right on City Boulevard. Go north to First Avenue and turn right again. Central Bank is on your right.*

   A: (Follows the directions on the map with a finger) *Thanks.*

5. Circulate during the activity to clarify directions and correct pronunciation.

Multilevel Option

Pre-level: Have pre-level pairs work together to create directions to different places on the map instead of taking turns to ask for and give directions.

Extension

After the class has finished the activity, have pairs choose a different starting point and continue the activity by asking for and giving directions from that point to other places on the map.

Variation

Have students write directions to places on the map. Have small groups of students read their directions aloud without giving the destinations. Group members should listen to the directions and identify the destinations.

Question and Answer Game: *How do I get there?*

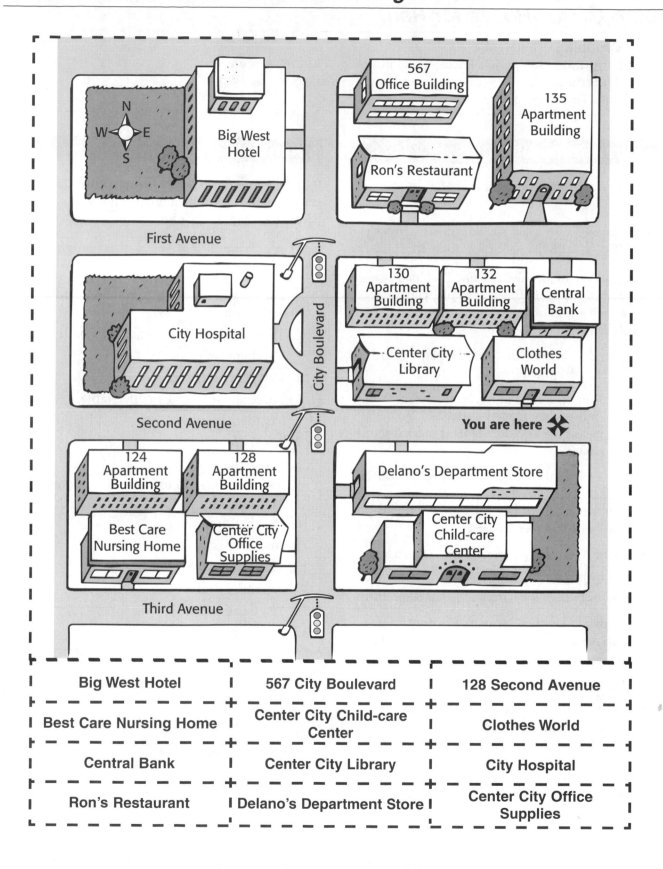

Board Game: *House for Rent*

Grouping	Groups of 4
Target Language	Rooms in a house, things in a room, *There is/There are*
Materials	Activity Master 30, a coin, and two markers for each group
Class Time	20 minutes

Teacher Preparation

Copy Activity Master 30, one for every four students.

Procedure

1. Put students in like-ability pairs. Each pair is a team. Put two teams together to play the game. Give each group of 4 a copy of Activity Master 30, a coin, and two markers.

2. Explain that students are going to play a board game. Here are the rules:

   • Pair 1 flips a coin to move. Heads means the team moves their marker ahead two squares; tails means the team moves their marker ahead one square.

   • Pair 1 moves the marker to a square. Student A reads the question aloud. Student B answers with true information. Pair 2 listens to make sure Pair 1's answer is correct.

   • If Pair 1's answer is correct, Pair 2 takes a turn.

   • If Pair 1's answer is incorrect, Pair 1 moves the marker back one square, and Pair 2 takes a turn.

   • If a pair lands on a square that already has a marker on it, the pair gets to move forward one square.

   • The first pair to reach FINISH wins.

3. Circulate during the activity to make sure students' answers are correct.

Extension

If some groups finish before the rest of the class, have students write lists of furniture the house needs. Then have pairs compare their lists.

Answer Key

1. There's a living room, a kitchen, and a bathroom.
2. There are two bedrooms and a bathroom.
3. No, there isn't.
4. There are four chairs.
5. There is a sofa and a coffee table.
6. No, there aren't.
7. Yes, there is.
8. Yes, there is.
9. It's one thousand four hundred dollars a month.
10. No, they aren't.
11. No, there isn't.
12. There are two bathrooms.
13. No, there isn't.
14. Yes, there is.
15. Yes, there are.

Board Game: *House for Rent*

START	1	2	3	4
FINISH	What's on the first floor? →	What's on the second floor? →	Is there parking? →	How many chairs are in the kitchen? ↓

15 Are there two closets in the large bedroom? ↑

5 What furniture is in the living room? ↓

14 Is there a yard? ↑

6 Are there closets in the small bedroom? ↓

13 Is there a refrigerator in the kitchen? ↑

Beautiful 2BR/2BA house for rent.
$1,400 a month (Utils. not incl.).
Some furniture, big yard.

7 Is there a sofa in the living room? ↓

12	11	10	9	8
How many bathrooms are there? ↑	Is there a shower on the second floor? ←	Are utilities included in the rent? ←	How much is the rent? ←	Is there a stove in the kitchen? ←

Information Gap: *Schedules*

Grouping Pairs
Target Language Simple present tense, questions with *What time*
Materials Activity Master 31
Class Time 20 minutes

Teacher Preparation

- Copy Activity Master 31, one for every two students.

- Cut out Schedules A and B. Clip together each set of schedules.

Procedure

1. Put students in like-ability pairs. Give a copy of Schedule A to Student A and a copy of Schedule B to Student B in each pair.

2. Explain that students are going to fill in the missing information in their schedules by asking each other: *What time does Betty _____?*

   Note: In their answers students will need to use *from . . . to* or *at* with the correct time expression.

3. On the board, write What time does Betty _____? Play the part of Student A. Call on an above-level student to play the part of Student B. Then model the activity:

   A: *What time does Betty have English class on Saturday?*

   B: *She has English class from 9:00 to 11:00 A.M.*

   A: *From 9:00 to 11:00 A.M.?*

   B: *Yes.*

   Instruct all Student As to write the time in their schedules.

4. Continue to model the activity:

   A: *What time does Betty meet friends for dinner on Saturday?*

   B: *She meets friends for dinner at 6:00 P.M.*

   A: *At 6:00 P.M.?*

   B: *Yes.*

   Instruct all Student As to write the time in their schedules.

5. To give students more support, write the model conversation on the board.

6. Have pairs continue the activity. Partners should take turns asking questions and filling in the times on their schedules.

7. Tell students not to show each other their schedules.

8. Circulate during the activity to help students form questions and to make sure they do not show their partners their schedules until the end of the activity. Make sure students are repeating the time to confirm it is correct.

9. After pairs have filled in all the blanks, have them compare schedules to check their information. The times on both schedules should be the same.

Multilevel Option

Pre-level: Give pre-level students some of the answers to write in their schedules so they have fewer questions to ask. For example, for Student A's, add *8:00 to 9:00 A.M.* (exercise) and for Student B's, add *12:00 to 5:00 P.M.* (work).

Extension

If some pairs finish before the rest of the class, have each student write his or her schedule for Saturday and Sunday. Then have students share their plans with their partners.

Information Gap: *Schedules*

Schedule A: Betty's Plans

Saturday	Sunday
_____ to _____ English class	_____ to _____ exercise
12:00 to 5:00 P.M. work	9:00 to 11:00 A.M. study English
_____ meet friends for dinner	_____ visit Aunt Rita
8:00 P.M. go to the movies	3:00 P.M. play soccer
	_____ to _____ babysit for Pam

Schedule B: Betty's Plans

Saturday	Sunday
9:00 to 11:00 A.M. English class	8:00 to 9:00 A.M. exercise
_____ to _____ work	_____ to _____ study English
6:00 P.M. meet friends for dinner	12:00 P.M. visit Aunt Rita
_____ go to the movies	_____ play soccer
	7:00 to 11:00 P.M. babysit for Pam

Unit 7 • Lesson 6

Future 1 pages 136–137

Build a Sentence: *Weekend Activities*

Grouping	Pairs
Target Language	Activities, adverbs of frequency, simple present tense
Materials	Activity Master 32
Class Time	20 minutes

Teacher Preparation

- Copy Activity Master 32, one for every two students.

- Cut each copy into 18 cards. Clip each set of cards together.

Procedure

1. Put students in like-ability pairs. Give each pair a set of cards.

2. Tell Student A to shuffle the cards. Have Student B put them faceup on his or her desk.

3. Explain that students are going to create true sentences about their weekend activities using the cards and then dictate them to their partners, who will write the questions in a notebook. Tell students they must include adverbs of frequency in their sentences.

4. Model the activity. Assemble a sentence and read it aloud: *I sometimes go to the beach on the weekend.*

   Note: The phrase *on the weekend* should be included in every sentence.

5. Write the sentence on the board. Tell students to assemble the sentence with their cards.

6. Tell students to continue to assemble correct sentences and write them down.

7. Circulate during the activity to make sure students' written sentences are correct.

Multilevel Options

Pre-level: Allow pre-level students to work together to create and write the sentences instead of taking turns for each task.

Above-level: Challenge above-level students to create sentences using different subject pronouns in order to practice verb conjugations. For example: *He usually does the laundry on the weekend.*

Extension

If some pairs finish before the rest of the class, have them write questions for each sentence they wrote. For example:

Sentence: I sometimes go to the beach on the weekend.

Question: How often do you go to the beach on the weekend?

Have students submit their questions to you for correction.

Answer Key

Possible sentences:

I never/sometimes/usually/always go to the beach on the weekend.

I never/sometimes/usually/always go to the park on the weekend.

I never/sometimes/usually/always go dancing on the weekend.

I never/sometimes/usually/always go swimming on the weekend.

I never/sometimes/usually/always do my homework on the weekend.

I never/sometimes/usually/always do the laundry on the weekend.

I never/sometimes/usually/always play cards on the weekend.

I never/sometimes/usually/always play basketball on the weekend.

I never/sometimes/usually/always play video games on the weekend.

---

64   Future 1 Multilevel Communicative Activities

Build a Sentence: *Weekend Activities*

I	to the beach	video games
go	to the park	always
do	dancing	sometimes
play	swimming	usually
cards	my homework	never
basketball	the laundry	on the weekend.

Picture-based Story: *Free Time*

Grouping	Pairs and then whole class
Target Language	Talking about how people spend their free time
Materials	Activity Master 33
Class Time	25 minutes

Teacher Preparation

Copy Activity Master 33, one for each student.

Procedure

1. Give a copy of Activity Master 33 to each student.

2. Explain that students are going to write a story based on the picture.

3. Put students in cross-ability pairs to discuss the questions on Activity Master 33.

4. Have students report their ideas to the class. Make sure students understand the scene: Anica isn't happy. Her husband Izaac goes jogging in his free time. Anica cleans the house in her free time.

5. Ask the class: *What's the story?* Have the class develop a story line orally.

6. Have students dictate the story line. Listen to students' ideas, repeat the ideas while rephrasing them in correct English, and write them on the board.

7. Have students copy the story into their notebooks.

Multilevel Option

Above-level: After they copy the story, have above-level students write comprehension questions about the story to ask the class.

Variation

Write the class story on an overhead projector transparency. This way you can photocopy the story for the following class and have students reread the text in pairs.

Extension

After the class has finished the activity, erase words from the story and have students tell you the missing words.

Picture-based Story: *Free Time*

PAIRS: Talk about the picture.

- How does Anica feel?
- What does she do in her free time?
- How does Izaac feel?
- What does he do in his free time?
- What happens next?

CLASS: Tell the story to the teacher.

Survey: *How often do you . . . ?*

Grouping	Whole-class mixer
Target Language	Adverbs of frequency, questions with *How often*
Materials	Activity Master 34
Class Time	20 minutes

Teacher Preparation

Copy Activity Master 34, one for each student.

Procedure

1. Give each student a copy of Activity Master 34.

2. Explain that students are going to walk around the classroom. They will ask and answer questions in order to complete the chart on Activity Master 34. Tell students they will have 15 minutes for the activity.

3. Write the following questions on the board:

   What activity do you do to relax?

   How often do you . . . ?

4. Walk around the classroom. Stop at the desk of an above-level student. Ask him or her to play the part of Student B. Then model the activity:

   A: *What activity do you do to relax?*

   B: (Names the activity)

   Write Student B's name and activity on the board.

5. Continue to model the acitvity:

   A: *How often do you _____?*

   B: (Responds using an adverb of frequency)

   Write Student B's answer on the board, next to his or her activity.

6. Continue to play the role of Student A. Walk around the classroom. Stop at the desk of another above-level student. Ask him or her to play the part of Student C. Ask Student C the questions on the board. Write Student C's answers on the board.

7. Circulate during the activity to help students ask the questions. Make sure they are transcribing their classmates' answers correctly.

Multilevel Options

Pre-level: During the activity, have pre-level students refer to the questions on the board.

Above-level: Challenge above-level students to do the activity without looking at the board.

Extension

After the class has finished the activity, have students look at the information in their survey and write sentences about their classmates on the board. For example:

Carlos goes to the park twice a week.

Mary knits three times a week.

Survey: *How often do you . . . ?*

Name	Activity	How often?

Board Game: *Daily Activities*

Grouping Groups of 4
Target Language Daily and free-time activities; adverbs of frequency; simple present questions with *When, What time,* and *How often*
Materials Activity Master 35, a coin, and two markers for each group
Class Time 20 minutes

Teacher Preparation

Copy Activity Master 35, one for every four students.

Procedure

1. Put students in like-ability pairs. Each pair is a team. Put two teams together to play the game. Give every four students a copy of Activity Master 35, a coin, and two markers.

2. Explain that students are going to play a board game. Here are the rules:

   • Pair 1 flips a coin to move. Heads means the team moves their marker ahead two squares; tails means the team moves their marker ahead one square.

   • Pair 1 moves the marker to a square. Student A forms the question, for example, *What time do you get up?* Student B answers with true information. Pair 2 listens to make sure Pair 1's question and answer are grammatically correct.

   • If Pair 1's question and answer are correct, Pair 2 takes a turn.

   • If Pair 1's question or answer is incorrect, Pair 1 moves their marker back one square, and Pair 2 takes a turn.

   • If a pair lands on a square that already has a marker on it, the pair gets to move forward one square.

   • The first pair to reach FINISH wins.

3. Circulate during the activity to make sure students' questions and answers are correct.

Extension

If some groups finish before the rest of the class, have students write a list of things they do once a week. Then have pairs compare their lists.

Board Game: *Daily Activities*

START	**1** When / exercise? →	**2** When / watch TV? →	**3** What time / go to sleep? ↓
7 What time / get up? ↓	**6** What time / eat dinner? ←	**5** How often / wash the dishes? ←	**4** What / usually / do / on the weekend? ←
8 When / shop for food? →	**9** How often / take a long walk? →	**10** What time / get home? →	**11** How often / watch TV? ↓
FINISH	**14** When / visit with family? ←	**13** How often / listen to music? ←	**12** What / usually / do / on Mondays? ←

Find Someone Who: *Do you like . . . ?*

Grouping Whole-class mixer
Target Language Foods, *yes/no* questions, count/non-count nouns
Materials Activity Master 36
Class Time 20 minutes

Teacher Preparation

Copy Activity Master 36, one for each student.

Procedure

1. Give each student a copy of Activity Master 36.

2. Explain that students are going to walk around the classroom. They will ask and answer *Do you like _____?* in order to complete as many sentences on Activity Master 36 as possible. Tell students they will have 15 minutes for the activity.

3. Write *Do you like _____?* on the board. Fill in the blank with the first item, *beans*. Then model the activity. Walk around the classroom, asking students *Do you like beans?* until you get a *yes* answer. Write the student's name to complete the first sentence on the Activity Master.

4. Circulate during the activity to help students formulate questions correctly.

Multilevel Option

Above-level: To increase the level of difficulty for above-level students, have them write two additional sentence prompts to extend the activity. For example:

_____ likes steak.

_____ likes cookies.

Extension

Put students in cross-ability pairs. Have each pair write on the board additional sentences about their classmates using the information they learned from this activity. For example:

Matt likes bananas.

Gelma likes cabbage.

After five minutes, have students go over their sentences with the class.

Variation

Have students do the activity in groups of 4. After five minutes, have students report to the class what they learned about their group members. The rest of the class listens and completes Activity Master 36.

Find Someone Who: *Do you like . . . ?*

Name	
	likes beans.
	likes bananas.
	likes cabbage.
	likes yogurt.
	likes pancakes.
	likes rice.
	likes pizza.
	likes pasta.
	likes scrambled eggs.
	likes cereal.
	likes fish.
	likes chicken.
	likes apples.

Picture-based Story: *Is the food fresh?*

Grouping	Pairs and then whole class
Target Language	Common foods, expiration dates
Materials	Activity Master 37
Class Time	25 minutes

Teacher Preparation

Copy Activity Master 37, one for each student.

Procedure

1. Give each student a copy of Activity Master 37.

2. Explain that students are going to write a story based on the picture.

3. Put students in cross-ability pairs to discuss the questions on Activity Master 37.

4. Have students report their ideas to the class. Make sure students understand the scene: The husband is throwing out the food because it is old. The wife is explaining to her mother that foods go bad, even in the refrigerator. She's explaining the dates on the food packages.

5. Ask the class: *What's the story?* Have the class develop a story line orally.

6. Have students dictate the story line. Listen to students' ideas, repeat the ideas while rephrasing them in correct English, and write them on the board.

7. Have students copy the story into their notebooks.

Multilevel Option

Above-level: After they copy the story, have above-level students write comprehension questions about the story to ask the class.

Variation

Write the class story on an overhead projector transparency. This way you can photocopy the story for the following class and have students reread the text in pairs.

Extension

After the class has finished the activity, erase words from the story and have students tell you the missing words.

Picture-based Story: *Is the food fresh?*

PAIRS: Talk about the picture.

• Why is the husband throwing out the food?

• What is the wife explaining to her mother?

CLASS: Tell the story to the teacher.

Role Play: *Can I help you?*

Grouping Groups of 3: one waiter and two customers
Target Language Ordering food from a menu
Materials Activity Master 38
Class Time 25 minutes

Teacher Preparation

Copy Activity Master 38, one for every three students.

Procedure

1. Give each group a copy of Activity Master 38.

2. Explain that groups of students are going to role-play ordering lunch at Jimmy's Restaurant. The rest of the class is going to listen to the role play and write down the order in their notebooks.

3. Write the model conversation on the board:

   A: Can I help you?

   B: Yes, I'd like a hamburger and a large order of fries.

   A: Anything else?

   B: No thanks.

   A: And you?

   C: I'd like a green salad.

   A: Large or small?

   C: Large, please.

4. Play the part of the waiter. Call on an above-level student to play the part of the customer. Take the student's order. Write his or her order on the board. Tell students to write the order in their notebooks.

5. Put students in cross-ability groups. Give the groups a few minutes to assign roles and read the menu.

6. One by one, invite the groups to the front of the class to present their role plays. After each role play, call on above-level students in the audience to retell each customer's order.

Multilevel Options

Pre-level: Allow pre-level students to look at the menu while they watch their classmates' role plays and check off the foods that the customers order.

Above-level: Tell above-level students to put the menus away while they watch their classmates' role plays. They must write their own notes on each customer's order.

Extension

Have pairs of students read the menu and answer the question below. They can share their answer with the class.

You have $8.00 for lunch. What can you get at Jimmy's Restaurant?

Role Play: *Can I help you?*

Jimmy's Restaurant

Lunch Menu

Sides
Chicken soup
Tomato and rice soup
Vegetable and bean soup

	cup	$3.00
	bowl	$4.00

Green salad

	small	$2.50
	large	$3.50

Sandwiches

Turkey	$4.00
Chicken	$4.10
Hamburger	$4.50

Extras

Lettuce, tomato, onion	15¢

Sides

Fries	small	$2.50
	large	$3.50

Desserts

Apple pie	$3.00
Fruit cup	$3.00
Ice cream	$3.00

Drinks

Juice (tomato, apple, or orange)	small	$2.50	large	$3.50
Milk	medium	$2.00	large	$2.50
Iced tea	medium	$1.75	large	$2.00
Soda	medium	$2.00	large	$3.00
Bottle of water	medium	$1.25	large	$2.50
Hot coffee / tea		$2.50		

Give and Take Game: *Shopping Lists*

Grouping	Whole-class mixer
Target Language	Common foods, *How many/How much*
Materials	Activity Master 39
Class Time	20 minutes

Teacher Preparation

• Copy Activity Master 39, one for every four students.

• Cut each Activity Master copy into 20 food cards and 4 shopping lists.

Procedure

1. Give each student five food cards and one shopping list at random.

2. Explain that students are going to get the foods on their lists. They must trade their food cards with their classmates to get the food cards they need.

3. Have students look through their food cards and check off any shopping list items that they already have. Have them set these cards aside.

4. Write on the board the following questions:

   Do you have any _____?

   How much do you have? How many do you have?

   Do you want _____ for your _____?

5. Play the role of Student A. Walk around the classroom. Stop at the desk of an above-level student. Ask him or her to play the part of Student B. Model the activity. For example:

   A: *I need two pounds of steak. Do you have steak?*

   B: *Yes, I do.*

   A: *How many pounds do you have?*

   B: *I have one pound.*

   A: *Do you want a pound of green beans for a pound of steak?*

   B: (Checks shopping list) *No thanks.*

   A: *How about a pound of pasta for a pound of steak?*

   B: (Checks shopping list) OK!

   A: (Trades the pasta food card for the pound of steak food card and checks off one of the two pounds of steak on her shopping list)

6. Circulate during the activity to help students negotiate.

Multilevel Option

Pre-level: To simplify the game, have pre-level students work together with one shopping list in a team of two.

Variation

Have students do the activity in groups of 4. Make sure each group is using the cards from the same copy of Activity Master 39.

Extension

If some students finish before the rest of the class, have them sit together in a group of 3 or 4. Have them plan a dinner for two people by using the foods on their shopping lists. Tell students they can add other foods if necessary.

Give and Take Game: *Shopping Lists*

1 lb. of steak	2 lbs. of rice	6 eggs	4 onions
1 lb. of steak	1 lb. of cheese	6 eggs	5 tomatoes
1 lb. of pasta	7 apples	6 eggs	5 oranges
1 lb. of pasta	5 potatoes	2 red peppers	5 oranges
1 lb. of turkey	5 potatoes	2 avocados	4 cucumbers

Shopping List
1 lb. of turkey
10 potatoes
4 cucumbers
7 apples

Shopping List
1 lb. of pasta
1 lb. of cheese
12 eggs
2 red peppers

Shopping List
2 lbs. of steak
1 lb. of pasta
5 tomatoes
2 avocados

Shopping List
2 lbs. of rice
4 onions
6 eggs
10 oranges

Board Game: *Food*

Grouping	Groups of 4
Target Language	Common foods, meals, restaurant foods, simple present questions
Materials	Activity Master 40, a coin, and two markers for each group
Class Time	20 minutes

Teacher Preparation

Copy Activity Master 40, one for every four students.

Procedure

1. Put students in like-ability pairs. Each pair is a team. Put two teams together to play the game. Give every four students a copy of Activity Master 40, a coin, and two markers.

2. Explain that students are going to play a board game. Here are the rules:

   • Pair 1 flips a coin to move. Heads means the team moves their marker ahead two squares; tails means the team moves their marker ahead one square.

   • Pair 1 moves the marker to a square. Student A asks the question. Student B answers with true information. Pair 2 listens to make sure Pair 1's answer is grammatically correct.

   • If Pair 1's answer is correct, Pair 2 takes a turn.

   • If Pair 1's answer is incorrect, Pair 1 moves the marker back one square, and Pair 2 takes a turn.

   • If a pair lands on a square that already has a marker on it, the pair gets to move forward one square.

   • The first pair to reach FINISH wins.

3. Circulate during the activity to make sure students' answers are correct.

Extension

If some groups finish before the rest of the class, have them write a list of foods in alphabetical order. For example:

apples

beans

carrots

Board Game: *Food*

START	**1** Do you like green beans? →	**2** How often do you eat fish? →	**3** What do you eat for breakfast? ↓
7 What do you eat for dinner? ↓	**6** Do you like coffee? ←	**5** Where do you keep milk? ←	**4** What food is better for your health—fried chicken or grilled chicken? ←
8 Where do you keep ice cream? →	**9** What food is better for your health—baked potatoes or fried potatoes? →	**10** Do you like apple pie? →	**11** How often do you eat cheese? ↓
FINISH	**14** How often do you eat rice? ←	**13** What do you eat for lunch? ←	**12** Do you like orange juice? ←

Picture Match: *Tell me about your picture.*

Grouping   Whole-class mixer
Target Language   Statements in the present continuous, weather vocabulary
Materials   Activity Master 41
Class Time   20 minutes

Teacher Preparation

- Copy Activity Master 41. Make enough copies so there will be one card for each student, plus extra cards for students who finish early.

- Cut each copy into four cards.

Procedure

1. Give one card to each student at random. Have students look at the picture of the woman on the card.

2. Explain that students are going to walk around the classroom. They will describe their pictures in order to find a matching card. Tell students not to show their cards to anyone. They will have 15 minutes for the activity.

3. Have students look at the pictures and identify the objects.

4. Play the part of Student A. Look at your card. Walk around the classroom. Ask an above-level student to play the part of Student B. Ask Student B to tell you about his or her picture. Continue to call on above-level students until you get a match.

5. To give students more support, write this model conversation on the board:

    A: Tell me about your picture.

    B: There's a woman. She's sitting in a chair.

    A: OK.

    B: It's snowing.

    A: Oh. In my picture it's sunny.

    Note: Remind students that they should continue to question students until they find a match.

6. Circulate during the activity to make sure students are not showing anyone their pictures and that they are forming correct sentences.

7. When students find a match, give them new cards so that they can continue the activity.

Multilevel Option

Pre-level: In order to support pre-level students in this activity, have all students spend two or three minutes writing sentences to describe their pictures before they talk to other classmates. During this preparation time, circulate to check the pre-level students' sentences for accuracy and vocabulary.

Extension

After the class has finished the activity, have students sit with a partner who has a different card. Have the pairs talk about how their two pictures are different. For example:

    A: *In my picture she's reading a book, but in your picture she's watching TV.*

    B: *In your picture it's cloudy, but in my picture it's sunny.*

Picture Match: *Tell me about your picture.*

Unit 9 • Lesson 6

Future 1 pages 176–177

Tic-Tac-Toe: *Present Continuous*

Grouping	Groups of 4
Target Language	Present continuous: *yes/no* questions and short answers
Materials	Activity Master 42
Class Time	20 minutes

Teacher Preparation

Copy Activity Master 42, one for every four students.

Procedure

1. Put students in like-ability pairs. Each pair is a team. Put two teams together to play the game. Give a copy of Activity Master 42 to every four students.

2. Explain that students are going to play Tic-Tac-Toe with true questions and answers about their classmates. Students on each team will create a correct question in the present continuous. The question must match a true answer in the grid. Here are the rules:

   • A student on Team A points to an answer in the grid (for example: *Yes, she is.*) and then asks a question (for example: *Is Jin-Hee playing a game?*). Since *Yes, she is* is the true answer, Team A marks an X over the answer in the grid.

   • Team B takes a turn by pointing to an answer and asking a question. If the question and answer are correct and true, Team B marks an O over the answer in the grid.

   • The first team to get three letters in a row— vertically, horizontally, or diagonally—wins.

3. Circulate during the activity to make sure students' questions are in the present continuous and grammatically correct, and that their answers are true.

4. Have students play a second round.

Multilevel Option

Above-level: Have above-level students write the questions while they play the game.

Extension

If some groups finish before the rest of the class, have each pair write questions for all the squares they did not win during the game. Have students submit their questions to you for correction.

84 Future 1 Multilevel Communicative Activities

Tic-Tac-Toe: *Present Continuous*

Round 1

No, she isn't.	Yes, she is.	No, they aren't.
No, I'm not.	No, he isn't.	Yes, we are.
No, you aren't.	No, we aren't.	Yes, you are.

Round 2

Yes, we are.	No, they aren't.	No, she isn't.
No, she isn't.	Yes, she is.	Yes, you are.
No, we aren't.	Yes, he is.	No, he isn't.

Picture-based Story: *Small Talk*

Grouping Pairs and then whole class
Target Language Small talk, weather
Materials Activity Master 43
Class Time 25 minutes

Teacher Preparation

Copy Activity Master 43, one for each student.

Procedure

1. Give each student a copy of Activity Master 43.

2. Explain that students are going to write a story based on the picture.

3. Put students in cross-ability pairs to discuss the questions on Activity Master 43.

4. Have students report their ideas to the class. Make sure students understand the scene: Mr. Sun and Ms. Gomez don't know each other. They start talking at the bus stop.

5. Ask the class: *What's the story?* Have the class develop a story line orally.

6. Have students dictate the story line. Listen to students' ideas, repeat the ideas while rephrasing them in correct English, and write them on the board.

7. Have students copy the story into their notebooks.

Multilevel Option

Above-level: After they copy the story, have above-level students write comprehension questions about the story to ask the class.

Variation

Write the class story on an overhead projector transparency. This way you can photocopy the story for the following class and have students reread the text in pairs.

Extension

After the class has finished the activity, erase words from the story and have students tell you the missing words.

Picture-based Story: *Small Talk*

PAIRS: Talk about the picture. Mr. Sun is waiting for the bus. Ms. Gomez is, too. They don't know each other.

• Describe the picture.

• What does Mr. Sun say to Ms. Gomez?

• What does Ms. Gomez say to Mr. Sun?

CLASS: Tell the story to the teacher.

Information Gap: *Weather Maps*

Grouping	Pairs
Target Language	Reading a weather map, weather vocabulary, adverbs of degree
Materials	Activity Master 44
Class Time	20 minutes

Teacher Preparation

- Copy Activity Master 44, one for every two students.
- Cut out Weather Maps A and B. Clip together each set of maps.

Procedure

1. Put students in like-ability pairs. Give a copy of Weather Map A to Student A and a copy of Weather Map B to Student B in each pair.

2. Explain that students are going to draw in the missing information in their weather maps by asking each other questions.

3. Go over the pronunciation of the names of the U.S. cities with the class.

4. On the board, write *How's the weather in* _____? Play the part of Student A. Call on an above-level student to play the part of Student B. Then model the activity:

   A: *How's the weather in Seattle?*

   B: *It's cool and rainy. It's 45 degrees.*

   A: *So in Seattle it's 45 degrees and rainy.*

   B: *Correct.*

   Instruct all Student As to draw the rain icon and write the temperature on their weather maps.

   Note: Each map has an example of all the weather icons. Encourage students to copy these icons.

5. To give students more support, write the model conversation on the board.

6. Have pairs continue the activity. Partners should take turns asking questions and filling in the information on their weather maps.

7. Tell students not to show each other their weather maps.

8. Circulate during the activity to make sure students do not show their partners their weather maps until the end of the activity. Make sure students repeat the weather information to confirm they understand.

9. After pairs have filled in all the blanks, have partners compare weather maps to check their information. The information on both weather maps should be the same.

Multilevel Option

Pre-level: Give pre-level students weather information to write on their maps so that they have fewer questions to ask. For example: Student As should add the sun icon and 75° to Los Angeles; Student Bs should add the cloud icon and 55° to San Francisco.

Extension

If some pairs finish before the rest of the class, have students write sentences about the weather in each city. Have them use the adverbs *very*, *pretty*, and *really*. For example:

> *It's very cold in Chicago. It's 20°, and it's snowing.*

Have students submit their sentences to you for correction.

Information Gap: *Weather Maps*

Weather Map A

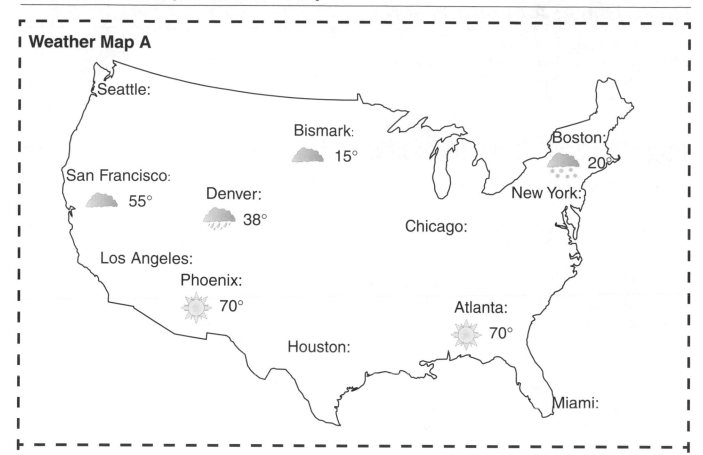

Seattle:

Bismark:
15°

Boston:
20°

San Francisco:
55°

Denver:
38°

New York:

Los Angeles:

Chicago:

Phoenix:
70°

Atlanta:
70°

Houston:

Miami:

Weather Map B

Seattle:
45°

Bismark:

Boston:

San Francisco:

New York:
35°

Denver:

Chicago:
20°

Los Angeles:
80°

Phoenix:

Atlanta:

Houston:
75°

Miami:
91°

Board Game: *Around the World*

Grouping Groups of 4
Target Language Present continuous questions and answers, adverbs of degree, weather
Materials Activity Master 45, a coin, two markers for each group
Class Time 20 minutes

Teacher Preparation

Copy Activity Master 45, one for every four students.

Procedure

1. Put students in like-ability pairs. Each pair is a team. Put two teams together to play the game. Give each group of 4 a copy of Activity Master 45, a coin, and two markers.

2. Explain that students are going to play a board game. Here are the rules:

   • Pair 1 flips a coin to move. Heads means the team moves their marker ahead two squares; tails means the team moves their marker ahead one square.

   • Pair 1 moves the marker to a square. Student A reads the question aloud. Student B answers with true information. Pair 2 listens to make sure Pair 1's answer is correct.

   • If Pair 1's answer is correct, Pair 2 takes a turn.

   • If Pair 1's answer is incorrect, Pair 1 moves the marker back one square, and Pair 2 takes a turn.

   • If a pair lands on a square that already has a marker on it, the pair gets to move forward one square.

   • The first pair to reach FINISH wins.

3. Circulate during the activity to make sure students' answers are correct.

Extension

If some groups finish before the rest of the class, have them write a weather report for Bangkok, Moscow, and Honolulu according to the pictures on the board game. Have students submit their weather reports to you for correction.

Answer Key

1. Peter is wearing earmuffs, a scarf, boots, a coat, and a hat.
2. It's hot and raining in Bangkok.
3. The Smiths are jogging on the beach.
4. It's winter in Moscow.
5. It's warm and sunny in Honolulu.
6. No, he isn't.
7. Vanida is walking.
8. It's cold and snowing in Moscow.
9. No, they aren't.
10. Vanida is wearing a dress and sandals.
11. No, it isn't pretty cool in Moscow. It's very cold.
12. No, she isn't.
13. The Smiths are wearing shorts, T-shirts, and sneakers.
14. Yes, it is.
15. Peter is standing at a bus stop.

Board Game: *Around the World*

| START / FINISH | 1 What is Peter wearing? → | 2 How is the weather in Bangkok? → | 3 What are the Smiths doing? → | 4 What season is it in Moscow? ↓ |

Vanida in Bangkok 90° F

Peter in Moscow 10° F

The Smith's in Honolulu 70° F

15 What is Peter doing? ↑

5 How is the weather in Honolulu? ↓

14 Is it very hot in Bangkok? ↑

6 Is Peter walking? ↓

13 What are the Smiths wearing? ↑

7 What is Vanida doing? ↓

12 Is Vanida talking on the phone? ↑

11 It is pretty cool in Moscow? ←

10 What is Vanida wearing? ←

9 Are the Smiths shopping? ←

8 How is the weather in Moscow? ←

Unit 10 • Lesson 3

aret Language Places in the community, prepositions of place
Materials Activity Master 46
Class Time 25 minutes

Teacher Preparation

Copy Activity Master 46, one for each student.

Procedure

1. Put students in like-ability pairs. Give each student a copy of Activity Master 46.

2. Hold up the Activity Master. Explain that students are going to fill in a community map. Students will first write the places in the community on their community map grids on Activity Master 46. Then they will describe the locations of the places to their partners, who will write what they hear without looking at their partner's map.

3. On the board, write the following prepositions of place from Units 3 and 10: next to, across from, around the corner from, down the block, between, on, and near.

4. Play the part of Student A. Call on an above-level student to play the part of Student B. Then model the activity. Write the names of places in your grid on Activity Master 46. Then draw an empty grid with the street names on the board and have Student B draw the places as you describe their location. For example:

   A: *The gas station is across from the police station.*

   B: *On 3rd Street?*

   A: *Yes. It's on the corner of 3rd Street and Central Avenue.*

   Student B writes *gas station* on the grid on the board.

   Note: Students may ask their partners to confirm the location, like Student B does above.

5. Give students five minutes to plan and fill in their own maps. Tell students not to show their maps to their partners.

6. Have students describe their maps to their partners. They will have a total of 15 minutes.

7. Circulate during the activity to help students ask clarifying questions when the maps don't match. For example: *Is the school between Lake Drive and Central Avenue?*

8. After 15 minutes, have partners compare their maps. The locations of the community places should be the same.

Multilevel Options

Pre-level: Allow pre-level students to look at and copy each other's maps. Then have them work together to write sentences about the locations of places on each map.

Above-level: Suggest that above-level students add two more community places to their maps, such as a drugstore and a coffee shop.

Extension

If some pairs finish before the rest of the class, have each student write sentences about his or her partner's map. Have students submit their writing to you for feedback. For example:

> The fire station is on the corner of 3rd Street and Lake Drive.
>
> The store is between the bank and the laundromat.

92 Future 1 Multilevel Communicative Activities

Drawing Game: *Community Map*

My Map

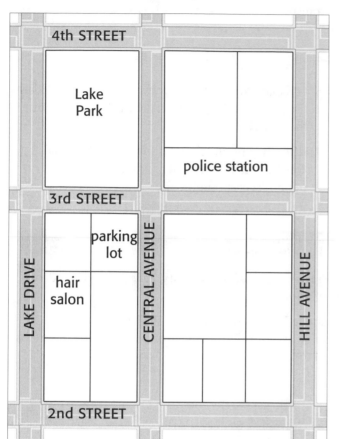

My Partner's Map

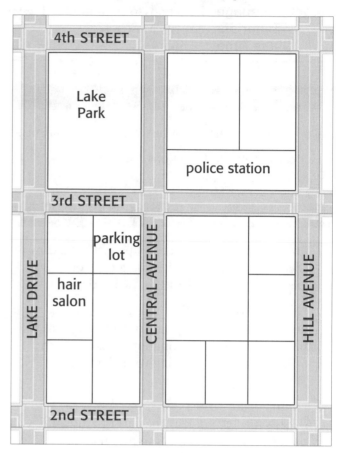

Places in the Community			
bank	fire station	gas station	laundromat
post office	school	store	supermarket

Information Gap: *Directions*

Grouping	Pairs
Target Language	Directions to community places; public transportation; questions with *How, How much, Where*
Materials	Activity Master 47
Class Time	20 minutes

Teacher Preparation

• Copy Activity Master 47, one for every two students.

• Cut each copy into Directions A and B.

Procedure

1. Put students in mixed-ability pairs. Give a copy of Directions A to Student A and a copy of Directions B to Student B in each pair.

2. Hold up a copy of Directions A. Point to the question box. Explain that students are going to fill in the missing information by asking each other questions beginning with *How . . .* , *Where . . .* , and *How much . . . .*

3. On the board write *How _____? Where _____? How much _____?* Play the part of Student A. Call on an above-level student to play the part of Student B. Then model the activity:

   A: *How do I get to City Hospital?*

   B: *Take the Number 3 subway.*

   Instruct all Student As to write *Number 3 subway* on the first line of item 1.

4. To give students more support, write the model conversation on the board.

5. Have pairs continue the activity. Partners should take turns asking the questions and completing the directions.

6. Circulate during the activity to make sure students do not show their partners their directions until the end of the activity.

7. After they fill in all the information, have pairs compare their directions. The information in both sets should be the same.

Multilevel Options

Pre-level: During the activity, have pre-level students refer to the question box.

Above-level: Tell above-level students to fold the question box under their cards and form the questions on their own.

Extension

If some pairs finish before the rest of the class, have students tell their partners how they get to the library, the hospital, the post office, or a nice park in their community.

Information Gap: *Directions*

Directions A

1. **To City Hospital**

   Take the _____.

   Get off at _____.

   Cost: _____

2. **To Central Library**

   Take the Number 89 bus.

   Get off at Center Street.

   Cost: $1.25

3. **To Lakeside Park**

   Take the Blue Line train.

   Get off at Pine Lake.

   Cost: $4.60

4. **To the main post office**

   Take the _____.

   Get off at _____.

   Cost: _____

> How do I get to . . . ?   Where do I get off?   How much does it cost?

Directions B

1. **To City Hospital**

   Take the Number 3 subway.

   Get off at Grove Avenue.

   Cost: $2.35

2. **To Central Library**

   Take the _____.

   Get off at _____.

   Cost: $_____

3. **To Lakeside Park**

   Take the _____.

   Get off at _____.

   Cost: _____

4. **To the main post office**

   Take the Number 21 bus.

   Get off at Grove Avenue.

   Cost: $1.70

> How do I get to . . . ?   Where do I get off?   How much does it cost?

Picture-based Story: *Excuse me. We're looking for . . .*

Grouping	Pairs and then whole class
Target Language	The library, asking for directions
Materials	Activity Master 48
Class Time	25 minutes

Teacher Preparation

Copy Activity Master 48, one for each student.

Procedure

1. Give each student a copy of Activity Master 48.

2. Explain that students are going to write a story based on the picture.

3. Put students in cross-ability pairs to discuss the questions on Activity Master 48.

4. Have students report their ideas to the class. Make sure students understand the scene: A mother and her son are at the public library. The son has some schoolwork. His mother is helping him. They are asking the librarian for help finding some materials.

5. Ask the class: *What's the story?* Have the class develop a story line orally.

6. Have students dictate the story line. Listen to students' ideas, repeat the ideas while rephrasing them in correct English, and write them on the board.

7. Have students copy the story into their notebooks.

Multilevel Option

Above-level: After they copy the story, have above-level students write comprehension questions about the story to ask the class.

Variation

Write the class story on an overhead projector transparency. This way you can photocopy the story for the following class and have students reread the text in pairs.

Extension

After the class has finished the activity, erase words from the story and have students tell you the missing words.

Picture-based Story: *Excuse me. We're looking for . . .*

PAIRS: Talk about the picture.

• Where are the mother and son?

• What are they doing?

• What are they looking for?

CLASS: Tell the story to the teacher.

Survey: *What are you doing this weekend?*

Grouping	Whole-class mixer
Target Language	Weekend plans, present continuous: questions and statements
Materials	Activity Master 49
Class Time	20 minutes

Teacher Preparation

Copy Activity Master 49, one for each student.

Procedure

1. Give each student a copy of Activity Master 49.

2. Explain that students are going to walk around the classroom. They will ask and answer questions in order to complete the chart on Activity Master 49. Tell students they will have 15 minutes for the activity.

3. Write the following question on the board:

   What are you doing this weekend?

4. Play the part of Student A. Walk around the classroom. Stop at the desk of an above-level student. Ask him or her to play the part of Student B. Then model the conversation:

   A: *What are you doing this weekend?*

   B: (States what he or she is doing this weekend, using the present continuous)

   Write Student B's name and his or her answer on the board.

5. Continue to play the role of Student A. Walk around the classroom. Stop at the desk of another above-level student. Ask him or her to play the part of Student C. Ask Student C what he or she is doing this weekend. Write Student C's answer on the board.

6. Circulate during the activity to help students ask the questions. Make sure they are transcribing their classmates' answers correctly.

Multilevel Options

Pre-level: During the activity, have pre-level students look at the board.

Above-level: Challenge above-level students to do the activity without looking at the board.

Extension

After the class has finished the activity, have students look at the information in their survey and write sentences about their classmates on the board. For example:

Meg is going dancing this weekend.

Joran is studying English this weekend.

Survey: *What are you doing this weekend?*

Name	Activity

Board Game: *Community and Transportation Map*

Grouping Groups of 4
Target Language Locations of places on a map, transportation routes and costs
Materials Activity Master 50, a coin, and two markers for each group
Class Time 20 minutes

Teacher Preparation

Copy Activity Master 50, one for every four students.

Procedure

1. Put students in like-ability pairs. Each pair is a team. Put two teams together to play the game. Give each group of 4 a copy of Activity Master 50, a coin, and two markers.

2. Explain that students are going to play a board game. Here are the rules:

 • Pair 1 flips a coin to move. Heads means the team moves their marker ahead two squares; tails means the team moves their marker ahead one square.

 • Pair 1 moves the marker to a square. Student A reads the question aloud. Student B answers with true information. Pair 2 listens to make sure Pair 1's answer is correct.

 • If Pair 1's answer is correct, Pair 2 takes a turn.

 • If Pair 1's answer is incorrect, Pair 1 moves the marker back one square, and Pair 2 takes a turn.

 • If a pair lands on a square that already has a marker on it, the pair gets to move forward one square.

 • The first pair to reach FINISH wins.

3. Circulate during the activity to make sure students' answers are correct.

Extension

If some groups finish before the rest of the class, have each student write a list of all the shops, stops, stations, and stores near his or her school. Then have students compare lists with their partners.

Answer Key

Sample answers:

1. We're on the corner of Pine Street and 8th Avenue.
2. The Glendale Supermarket is on River Parkway between 6th and 7th Avenues.
3. Yes, it is.
4. Yes, there's a gas station on the corner of Murray Street and 8th Avenue.
5. No, it isn't. It's between 6th and 7th Avenues.
6. Go north on Pine Street. Turn right on 4th Avenue. The post office is on the corner of Murray Street and 4th Avenue.
7. The police station is on Murray Street between 5th and 6th Avenues.
8. Get the Number 101 bus on the corner of Murray Street and 4th Avenue.
9. The fire station is on the corner of Pine Street and Eighth Avenue.
10. Yes, there's a coffee shop on the corner of River Parkway and 7th Avenue.
11. National Bank is on Pine Street between 4th and 5th Avenues.
12. Go north on Pine Street. Saint Luke's Hospital is between 3rd and 4th Avenues.
13. Glendale Park is on Pine Street between 5th and 6th Avenues.
14. Get the Number 95 bus on the corner of Pine Street and 3rd Avenue.
15. A hair salon is on the corner of 3rd Avenue and River Parkway.

Board Game: *Community and Transportation Map*

START	1 Where are we? →	2 Where's the Glendale Super-market? →	3 Is DVS Drugstore across the street from the post office? →	4 Is there a gas station in Glendale? ↓
FINISH				

| 15 What is on the corner of 3rd Avenue and River Parkway? ↑ | | | | 5 Is Stacey's Department Store between 4th and 5th Avenues? ↓ |

3rd Avenue
Hair Salon   Bus Stop   Saint Luke's Hospital   DVS Drugstore
4th Avenue
National Bank   Post Office   Bus Stop
5th Avenue
Glendale Park   Police Station
6th Avenue
Glendale Supermarket   Stacy's Department Store
7th Avenue
Coffee Shop   Fire Station   Gas Station
8th Avenue
YOU ARE HERE

River Parkway · Pine Street · Elm Street · Murray Street · #95

| 14 Where do you get the Number 95 bus? ↑ | | | | 6 How do you get to the post office? ↓ |

| 13 Where's Glendale Park? ↑ | | | | 7 Where's the police station? ↓ |

| 12 How do you get to Saint Luke's Hospital? ↑ | 11 Where's National Bank? ← | 10 Is there a coffee shop around here? ← | 9 What is on the corner of Pine Street and 8th Avenue? ← | 8 Where do you get the Number 101 bus? ← |

Miming Game: *What's wrong?*

Grouping Pairs
Target Language Health problems, *yes/no* questions in simple present
Materials Activity Master 51
Class Time 15 minutes

Teacher Preparation

- Copy Activity Master 51, one for each pair.

- Cut the copies into 12 cards and clip each set together.

Procedure

1. Put students in like-ability pairs. Give each pair a set of cards.

2. Explain that students are going to take turns picking up a card and miming the health problem on the card. Their partners guess the problem.

3. Play the part of Student A. Call on an above-level student to play the part of Student B. Then model the activity. For example:

   A: (Picks up a card and begins to mime pain in the ear)

   B: *Does your head hurt?*

   A: *No, it doesn't.* (Continues to mime ear pain)

   B: *Do you have an earache?*

   A: *Yes, I do.*

4. Circulate during the activity to help students formulate complete questions.

Multilevel Option

Above-level: Have above-level students write a sentence after they guess their partner's health problem. For example:

   Ngyugen has an earache.

Extension

If some pairs finish before the rest of the class, have partners work together to write a list of all the body parts they can remember without looking at their Student Book. Have pairs submit their lists to you for spelling corrections.

Variation

Have students do the activity in groups of 4.

Miming Game: *What's wrong?*

You have a headache.	You have a toothache.
You have a sore throat.	You have a fever.
You have an earache.	You have a cough.
You have a stuffy nose.	You have a stomachache.
Your back hurts.	Your shoulder hurts.
Your neck hurts.	Your knee hurts.

Unit 11 • Lesson 4

Future 1 pages 211–213

Picture-based Story: *I'd like to make an appointment.*

Grouping Pairs and then whole class
Target Language Health problems, making a doctor's appointment
Materials Activity Master 52
Class Time 25 minutes

Teacher Preparation

Copy Activity Master 52, one for each student.

Procedure

1. Give each student a copy of Activity Master 52.

2. Explain that students are going to write a story based on the picture.

3. Put students in cross-ability pairs to discuss the questions on Activity Master 52.

4. Have students report their ideas to the class. Make sure students understand the scene: A mother is worried about her daughter. The girl is very sick and has a fever. The mother calls the doctor's office to make an appointment.

5. Ask the class: *What's the story?* Have the class develop a story line orally.

6. Have students dictate the story line. Listen to students' ideas, repeat the ideas while rephrasing them in correct English, and write them on the board.

7. Have students copy the story into their notebooks.

Multilevel Option

Above-level: After they copy the story, have above-level students write comprehension questions about the story to ask the class.

Variation

Write the class story on an overhead projector transparency. This way you can photocopy the story for the following class and have students reread the text in pairs.

Extension

After the class has finished the activity, erase words from the story and have students tell you the missing words.

Picture-based Story: *I'd like to make an appointment.*

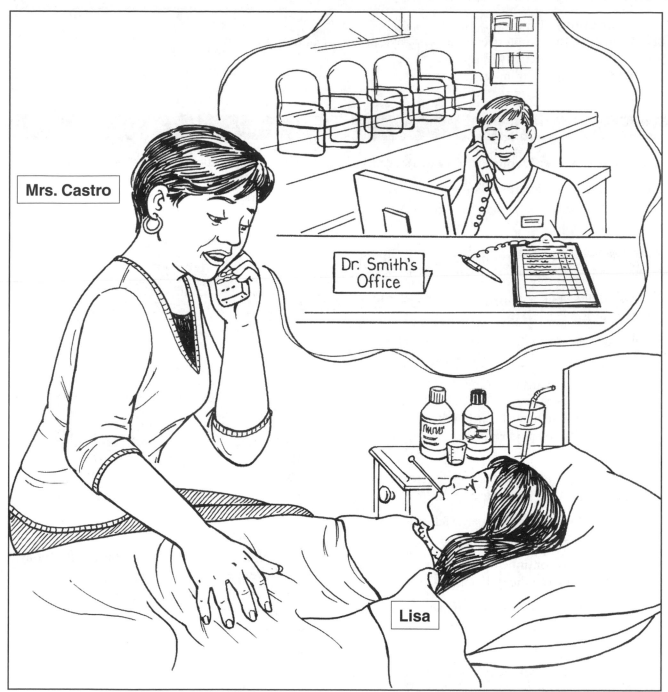

PAIRS: Talk about the picture.

• How does the daughter, Lisa, feel?

• What are Mrs. Castro and the office assistant talking about?

• What happens next?

CLASS: Tell the story to the teacher.

Build a Sentence: *Yesterday and Today*

Grouping   Pairs
Target Language   Simple present tense, simple past tense of *to be* and *to have*
Materials   Activity Master 53
Class Time   15 minutes

Teacher Preparation

- Copy Activity Master 53, one for every two students.

- Cut each copy into 15 cards. Clip each set of cards together.

Procedure

1. Put students in like-ability pairs. Give each pair a set of cards.

2. Tell Student A to shuffle the cards. Have Student B put them faceup on his or her desk.

3. Explain that students are going to take turns creating sentences using the cards and dictating them to their partner, who will write the sentences in a notebook. Tell students there is a total of 16 possible sentences.

4. Model the activity. Assemble a sentence and read it aloud: *They were sick yesterday.*

5. Write the sentence on the board. Tell students to assemble the sentence with their cards.

6. Tell students to continue to assemble correct sentences and write them down.

7. Circulate during the activity to make sure students' written sentences are correct.

Multilevel Option

Pre-level: Allow pre-level students to work together to create and write the sentences instead of taking turns.

Extension

If some pairs finish before the rest of the class, have them find the seven cards with verbs. Then have partners work together to write sentences using each verb. For example:

> *We are in class today.*

> *I had a sore throat yesterday.*

Have students submit their sentences to you for your feedback.

Answer Key

Possible sentences:

They are sick today.	He is sick today.
They were sick yesterday.	He was sick yesterday.
They are absent today.	He is absent today.
They were absent yesterday.	He was absent yesterday.
They have the flu today.	He has the flu today.
They had the flu yesterday.	He had the flu yesterday.
They are better today.	He is better today.
They were better yesterday.	He was better yesterday.

Build a Sentence: *Yesterday and Today*

They	is	sick
He	are	the flu
was	has	absent
were	have	yesterday.
better	had	today.

Interview: *What's your advice?*

Grouping	Pairs
Target Language	Giving advice with *should*, talking about medical problems
Materials	Activity Master 54
Class Time	25 minutes

Teacher Preparation

Copy Activity Master 54, one for each student.

Procedure

1. Put students in like-ability pairs. Give each student a copy of Activity Master 54.

2. Explain that students are going to interview their partners, asking for their advice.

3. Play the part of Student A. Call on an above-level student to play the part of Student B. Then model the activity. For example:

   A: *What's your advice for a person with a cold?*

   B: *Take a pain reliever.*

   A: (Writes Student B's answer) *Anything else?*

   B: *Drink a lot of water.*

   A: (Writes Student B's answer)

   Note: After Student B finishes answering the questions, he or she should ask Student A for his or her advice.

4. Circulate during the activity to help students with vocabulary questions. Write the new words on the board.

Multilevel Options

Pre-level: Encourage pre-level students to refer to the vocabulary box for words and ideas.

Above-level: Have above-level students fold the vocabulary box under the page and give advice using their own words.

Extension

If some students finish before the rest of the class, have partners ask each other how often they experience the medical problems on Activity Master 54. For example:

   A: *How often do you get a cold?*

   B: *Not often. I get a cold once a year. How about you?*

Interview: *What's your advice?*

What's your advice for a person with . . .	
1. a cold?	
2. a sore throat?	
3. a fever?	
4. a stuffy nose?	
5. an earache?	
6. a headache?	
7. a lot of stress?	

drink _____	eat _____	exercise
drink tea and honey	stay in bed	take a deep breath
go to the doctor	take a hot shower	take a pain reliever
take a fever reducer	use an ice pack	use a heating pad

Board Game: *Follow the instructions.*

Grouping Groups of 4
Target Language Medical instructions, parts of the body
Materials Activity Master 55, a coin, and two markers for each group
Class Time 20 minutes

Teacher Preparation

Copy Activity Master 55, one for every four students.

Procedure

1. Put students in like-ability pairs. Each pair is a team. Put two teams together to play the game. Give every four students a copy of Activity Master 55, a coin, and two markers.

2. Explain that students are going to play a board game. Here are the rules:

   • Pair 1 flips a coin to move. Heads means the team moves their marker ahead two squares; tails means the team moves their marker ahead one square.

   • Pair 1 moves the marker to a square. Student A reads the instructions to Student B who acts it out. Pair 2 watches to make sure Pair 1's pronunciation of the instruction and response are correct.

   • If Pair 1's response is correct, Pair 2 takes a turn.

   • If Pair 1's response is incorrect, Pair 1 moves the marker back one square, and Pair 2 takes a turn.

   • If a pair lands on a square that already has a marker on it, the pair gets to move forward one square.

   • The first pair to reach FINISH wins.

3. Circulate during the activity to make sure students' answers are correct.

Extension

If some groups finish before the rest of the class, have them write a list of body parts that come in pairs and a list of body parts that are singular. Have students submit their writing to you for spelling corrections. For example:

Singular: head, neck, back

Pairs: eyes, ears, feet

Board Game: *Follow the instructions.*

START	**1** Shake your head. →	**2** Touch your ankles. →	**3** Look straight ahead. ↓
7 Take a deep breath. ↓	**6** Roll up your sleeve. ←	**5** Make a fist. ←	**4** Open your mouth. ←
8 Shake a leg. →	**9** Say *Ahh.* →	**10** Sit on the table. →	**11** Touch your nose. ↓
FINISH	**14** Nod your head. ←	**13** Touch your shoulder. ←	**12** Clap your hands. ←

Interview: *Skill Inventory*

Grouping Pairs
Target Language Identify job skills, *can* for ability
Materials Activity Master 56
Class Time 20 minutes

Teacher Preparation

Copy Activity Master 56, one for each student.

Procedure

1. Put students in like-ability pairs and give each student a copy of Activity Master 56.

2. Explain that students are going to complete the inventory about their own skills and then talk to their partners about their skills. Tell students they will have five minutes to complete their inventories and ten minutes to talk with and listen to their partners.

3. Model the activity. Read through the first few items on the list aloud and mark a check ✓ for the skills you have and an X for the skills you don't. Then invite an above-level student up to the front of the class to play the part of Student B. Give the student an extra Activity Master. Play the part of Student A and tell Student B about your skills without showing your list. Student B listens and marks your skills on his or her Activity Master. For example:

   A: *I can use a computer and make copies on a photocopy machine. I can drive a car, but I can't drive a truck.*

   B: (Marks a ✓ on items 1, 2, and 3, and marks an X next to item 4, in the column *My Partner.*) *Excuse me, you can or can't drive a car?*

   A: *I can.*

   B: (Marks a ✓ on number 4.)

   Note: After Student A finishes explaining all of his or her skills, Student B can begin.

4. Circulate during the activity to make sure students listen to one another and complete the information about their partner's skills without looking at their partner's Activity Master.

Multilevel Options

Pre-level: Have pairs work together to read each line and check the columns.

Above-level: To increase the level of difficulty for above-level pairs, have students add two skills to the list.

Extension

After the class has finished the activity, have students circle the skills they don't have but want to learn. Ask students to tell the class three skills they want to learn.

Interview: *Skill Inventory*

Skill	Me	My Partner
I can . . .	Yes ✓ No X	Yes ✓ No X
1. use a computer.		
2. make copies on a photocopy machine.		
3. drive a car.		
4. drive a truck.		
5. fix sinks and toilets.		
6. fix cars.		
7. cook good food.		
8. make desserts.		
9. take care of very young children.		
10. lift heavy boxes.		
11. take care of building grounds.		
12. speak two languages.		
13. use a cash register.		
14. take phone messages in English.		
15.		
16.		

Job Match: *Tell me about your skills.*

Grouping	Whole-class mixer
Target Language	Job skills, schedule availability, questions and short answers with *can*
Materials	Activity Master 57
Class Time	20 minutes

Teacher Preparation

- Copy Activity Master 57. Make enough copies so there will be one card for each student, plus extra cards for students who finish early.

- Cut the copy into 20 cards.

Procedure

1. Give each student a card at random. Have students read the information on their cards.

2. Explain that students are going to do short job interviews. The employers will sit at their desks, and the applicants will move around the classroom looking for a job that matches their skills. Tell students not to show their cards to anyone. They will have 15 minutes for the activity.

   Note: The white cards are for the employers, and the shaded cards are for the applicants.

3. Write the following lines on the board:

   Applicant

   I'm looking for a job.

   I can _____.

   Employer

   Tell me about your skills.

   I'm looking for a _____.

   Can you work _____?

4. Play the part of Student B, the employer. Look at your card. Walk around the classroom. Ask an above-level student to play the part of Student A, an applicant. Ask the questions on the board. Continue to call on above-level students until you get a match.

5. To give students more support, write this model conversation on the board:

   A: Hello. I'm looking for a job.

   B: OK. Tell me about your skills.

   A: Well, I can drive a truck. I can lift heavy things.

   B: Hmm. I'm looking for a truck driver. Can you work Monday to Friday?

   A: No, I can't. I can only work weekends.

   B: Too bad. This job is for Monday to Friday.

   Note: Remind students that they should continue to question students until they find a match.

6. Circulate during the activity to make sure students are not showing anyone their cards. When students find a job match, give each another card to continue the game.

Multilevel Options

Pre-level and above-level: Hand out white cards to above- and on-level students and shaded cards to pre-level students.

Extension

After the class has finished the activity, have students work with their final partners to write out their interviews. Have students submit their writing to you for feedback.

Job Match: *Tell me about your skills.*

Help Wanted: Delivery Person Schedule: Monday–Friday	Skills: can drive a truck can lift heavy boxes Availability: Monday–Friday only
Help Wanted: Delivery person Schedule: Weekend evenings 5:00 P.M.–Midnight	Skills: can drive a truck can lift heavy boxes Availability: evenings and weekends only
Help Wanted: Gardener Schedule: Monday–Saturday 9:00–4:00	Skills: can lift heavy things can take care of grounds Availability: 7 days a week, after 9:00 A.M.
Help Wanted: Gardener Schedule: Tuesday–Friday 6:00 A.M.–5:00 P.M.	Skills: can lift heavy things can take care of grounds Availability: Tuesday–Sunday
Help Wanted: Cashier Schedule: Sunday–Thursday 6:00 P.M. to 11:00 P.M. shift	Skills: can use a cash register can take returns Availability: evenings only
Help Wanted: Cashier Schedule: Monday–Thursday 8:00 A.M. to 4:00 P.M.	Skills: can use a cash register can take returns Availability: Monday–Friday only
Help Wanted: Office Assistant Schedule: Monday–Friday 9:00–5:00	Skills: can use a computer can answer phones/take messages Availability: Monday–Friday only
Help Wanted: Office Assistant Schedule: Monday–Saturday 8:00 A.M.–noon	Skills: can use a computer can answer phones/take messages Availability: mornings only
Help Wanted: Child-care Worker Schedule: Monday–Friday 8:00 A.M. to 3:00 P.M.	Skills: can take care of very young children can drive a car Availability: mornings and afternoons
Help Wanted: Child-care Worker Schedule: Weekend evenings 5:00 P.M.–Midnight	Skills: can take care of very young children can cook well Availability: weekends only

Unit 12 • Lesson 7

Picture-based Story: *Robson's Interview*

Grouping	Pairs
Target Language	Job interview, body language
Materials	Activity Master 58
Class Time	25 minutes

Teacher Preparation

Copy Activity Master 58, one for each student.

Procedure

1. Give each student a copy of Activity Master 58.

2. Explain that students are going to write a story based on the pictures.

3. Put students in cross-ability pairs to discuss the questions on Activity Master 58.

4. Have students report their ideas to the class. Make sure students understand the scene: Robson is applying for a job. He doesn't have a good interview. He doesn't get the job. He goes to a job counselor to get tips on how to get a job.

5. Ask the class: *What's the story?* Have the class develop a story line orally.

6. Have students dictate the story line. Listen to students' ideas, repeat the ideas while rephrasing them in correct English, and write them on the board.

7. Have students copy the story into their notebooks.

Multilevel Option

Above-level: After they copy the story, have above-level students write comprehension questions about the story to ask the class.

Variation

Write the class story on an overhead projector transparency. This way you can photocopy the story for the following class and have students reread the text in pairs.

Extension

After the class has finished the activity, erase words from the story and have students tell you the missing words.

Picture-based Story: *Robson's Interview*

a.

b.

c.

d.

PAIRS: Talk about each picture.

- What is Robson doing in each picture?
- Does Robson get the job? Why or why not?
- What does Robson learn in the job counselor's class?
- What happens next?

CLASS: Tell the story to the teacher.

Information Gap: *Maria's Job History*

Grouping	Pairs
Target Language	*Be*: simple past questions, possessive nouns, questions with *who*
Materials	Activity Master 59
Class Time	20 minutes

Teacher Preparation

- Copy Activity Master 59, one for every two students.

- Cut each copy in half. Clip together each set of job applications.

Procedure

1. Put students in like-ability pairs. Give a copy of Job Application A to Student A and a copy of Job Application B to Student B in each pair.

2. Explain that students are going to fill in the missing information in their job applications by asking each other questions.

3. Play the part of Student A. Call on an above-level student to play the part of Student B. Then model the activity:

   A: *What is Maria's job?*

   B: *Maria is an office assistant.*

   Instruct all Student As to write the phrase *office assistant* in the correct place on the application.

4. Continue to model the activity. Instruct Student B to continue the conversation:

   A. *What are Maria's job duties?*

   B. *Make copies, use a computer, and answer phones.*

   Instruct all Students Bs to write the phrase *make copies, use a computer, answer phones* in the correct place on the application.

5. To give students more support, write the model conversation on the board.

6. Have pairs continue the activity. Partners should take turns asking about the information missing from their job applications.

7. Tell students not to show each other their copies of the job application.

8. Circulate during the activity to help students with pronunciation and to make sure they do not show their partners their job applications until the end of the activity.

9. When pairs have filled in all the information, have partners compare job applications to check their information. The information on both applications should be the same.

Multilevel Options

Pre-level: Have pre-level students refer to the question box on their card.

Above-level: Have above-level students fold the question box under their card and form the questions on their own.

Extension

If some pairs finish the activity before the rest of the class, have partners work together to write sentences about Maria to submit to you for your correction. For example:

Maria is an office assistant.

She makes copies, uses a computer, and answers the phone.

Information Gap: *Maria's Job History*

Job Application A

Job History: (list most recent first)

Company <u>Medical Associates</u>

Job _____

Circle one: Full-time   Part-time

From <u>8/15/09</u> To <u>now</u>

Duties <u>make copies, use computer,</u>
<u>answer phone</u>

Pay <u>$14/hour</u>

Company <u>Clothing World</u>

Job <u>sales assistant</u>

Circle one: (Full-time)   Part-time

From _____ To _____

Duties _____

_____

Pay <u>$10/hour</u>

> What is Maria's job?   Is her job full-time or part-time?
>
> When was she at her last job?   What were her job duties at her last job?

Job Application B

Job History: (list most recent first)

Company <u>Medical Associates</u>

Job <u>office assistant</u>

Circle one: Full-time   (Part-time)

From <u>8/15/09</u> To <u>now</u>

Duties _____

_____

Pay _____

Company <u>Clothing World</u>

Job _____

Circle one: Full-time   Part-time

From <u>8/15/07</u> To <u>8/15/09</u>

Duties <u>help customers, use cash</u>
<u>register</u>

Pay <u>$10/hour</u>

> What are Maria's job duties?   What is her pay?
>
> What was her last job?   Was her last job full-time or part-time?

Board Game: *Job Skills and History*

Grouping	Groups of 4
Target Language	*Be:* simple past, *can* for ability, job skills and job history
Materials	Activity Master 60, a coin, and two markers for each group
Class Time	20 minutes

Teacher Preparation

Copy Activity Master 60, one for every four students.

Procedure

1. Put students in like-ability pairs. Each pair is a team. Put two teams together to play the game. Give every four students a copy of Activity Master 60, a coin, and two markers.

2. Explain that students are going to play a board game. Here are the rules:

   • Pair 1 flips a coin to move. Heads means the team moves their marker ahead two squares; tails means the team moves their marker ahead one square.

   • Pair 1 moves the marker to a square. Student A reads the question aloud. Student B answers with true information. Pair 2 listens to make sure Pair 1's answer is correct.

   • If Pair 1's answer is correct, Pair 2 takes a turn.

   • If Pair 1's answer is incorrect, Pair 1 moves the marker back one square, and Pair 2 takes a turn.

   • If a pair lands on a square that already has a marker on it, the pair gets to move forward one square.

   • The first pair to reach FINISH wins.

3. Circulate during the activity to make sure students' answers are correct.

Multilevel Option

Pre-level: To make the game easier, allow each pair to rehearse the question-and-answer conversation before they perform it for the other pair.

Extension

If some groups finish the game before the rest of the class, have each pair write sentences using information they learned during the game about the two students in their opposing team. For example:

> Phat can answer phones and take messages in English.

> Amelie was at her last job for three years.

Board Game: *Job Skills and History*

START	**1** What do you do? →	**2** What are the job duties of an office assistant? →	**3** Can you take care of young children? ↓
7 Do you have a part-time job? ↓	**6** Can you lift heavy things? ←	**5** What hours can you work? ←	**4** Can you drive a car? ←
8 What was your last job? →	**9** How long were you at your last job? →	**10** How do you make a good impression in a job interview? (Give three tips.) →	**11** What are the job duties of a sales assistant? ↓
FINISH	**14** Can you answer phones and take messages in English? ←	**13** What are the job duties of a delivery person? ←	**12** Can you speak two languages? ←